JIM ROHN'S

SUCCESS
BLUEPRINT

AN OFFICIAL NIGHTINGALE-CONANT PUBLICATION

JIM ROHN'S

SUCCESS BLUEPRINT

TIMELESS PRINCIPLES FOR SHAPING YOUR FUTURE

JIM ROHN

Published and distributed by:
SOUND WISDOM
P.O. Box 310
Shippensburg, PA 17257-0310
717-530-2122

info@soundwisdom.com

www.soundwisdom.com

Manuscript developed from *The Ultimate Jim Rohn Library* (Nightingale-Conant)

While efforts have been made to verify information contained in this publication, neither the author nor the publisher assumes any responsibility for errors, inaccuracies, or omissions. While this publication is chock-full of useful, practical information; it is not intended to be legal or accounting advice. All readers are advised to seek competent lawyers and accountants to follow laws and regulations that may apply to specific situations. The reader of this publication assumes responsibility for the use of the information. The author and publisher assume no responsibility or liability whatsoever on the behalf of the reader of this publication.

ISBN 13 TP: 978-1-64095-493-9

ISBN 13 eBook: 978-1-64095-494-6

For Worldwide Distribution, Printed in the U.S.A.

1 2 3 4 5 6 7 8 / 29 28 27 26 25

CONTENTS

FOREWORD

The Nightingale-Conant Corporation is proud to present *Jim Rohn's Success Blueprint,* which has been taken in part from the "Ultimate Jim Rohn Library audio collection," priceless wisdom preserved in sound by one of the greatest personal development speakers and philosophers in history.

Emanuel James (Jim) Rohn was born in Yakima, Washington to Emanuel and Clara Rohn. The Rohns owned and worked a farm in Caldwell, Idaho, where Jim grew up as an only child. Rohn started his professional life by working as a stock clerk for a department store, Sears. Around this time a friend invited him to a lecture given by entrepreneur John Earl Shoaff.

In 1955, Rohn joined Shoaff's direct-selling business AbundaVita as a distributor. In 1957, Rohn resigned his distributorship with AbundaVita and joined Nutri-Bio, another direct-selling company. It was at this point that the company's founders, including Shoaff, started to mentor him. After this mentorship, Rohn built one of the largest organizations in the company. In 1960 when Nutri-Bio expanded into Canada, Shoaff and the other founders selected Rohn as a vice president for the organization.

In the early 1960s, Rohn was invited to speak at a meeting of his rotary club. He accepted, and soon others began asking him to speak at various luncheons and other events. In 1963 at the Beverly Hills Hotel, he gave his first public seminar. He then began presenting seminars across the United States, telling his story and teaching his personal development philosophy.

Throughout the 1970s, Rohn conducted a number of seminars for Standard Oil. At the same time, he participated in a personal development business called Adventures and Achievement, which featured both live seminars as well as personal development workshops. He presented seminars worldwide for more than 40 years.

In the last part of the 1970s, Rohn mentored Mark R. Hughes, the founder of Herbalife International, and motivational speaker Tony Robbins. In fact, a young Tony Robbins could be found in the back of the room at many of Jim Rohn's seminars, and he actually ran one of Jim Rohn's offices in his early years.

Others who credit Rohn for his influence on their careers include authors Mark Victor Hansen and Jack Canfield of the *Chicken Soup for the Soul* book series; authors and lecturers Brian Tracy, Todd Smith, and T. Harv Eker. Rohn also co-authored the novel *12 Pillars* with Chris Widener.

Rohn was the recipient of the 1985 National Speakers Association, CPAE Award for Excellence in Speaking. He also authored 17 various written audio and video media. The world lost one of its most inspirational leaders and speakers when Jim Rohn died in 2009.

In this book you will read some of his most dynamic stories, practical advice, and success secrets. Legendary speaker and co-founder of Nightingale-Conant, Mr. Earl Nightingale, called Jim Rohn "the most powerful results-oriented leader and speaker of our time." His philosophy of personal responsibility is the foundation that underlays every major topic that Jim Rohn ever discussed—the fact that you are 100 percent responsible to navigate your future to reap the results you achieve in your life. Jim discusses the major determining factors in how your life works out and how to develop the ambition you need to propel you to greater success.

Nightingale-Conant

1

SETTING YOUR SAILS

As mentioned in the Foreword, your personal philosophy is the major determining factor in how your life works out. To form a philosophy, you have to think, you have to use your mind. You have to process ideas—and this whole process continues over your lifetime.

Developing our personal view of life started way back when we were children, the schools we attended, our parents and family, our friends, our experiences, everything we accumulate over the years, day by day. And it includes how you set the sail. Each person's personal philosophy is like setting your sail to catch the favorable winds that will carry you to your desired destination. Setting your sail also includes your attitude and response to challenges, those troublesome winds of adversity.

I used to think that circumstances beyond my control ordered my life. If someone would've asked me at age 25, "Mr. Rohn, why aren't you doing very well in life? You have only pennies in your pocket, creditors calling, nothing in the bank, and you're behind on your promises to your family. You live in America, you're 25 years old, you have a beautiful family and every reason to do well...yet things are not going that well for you. What's wrong?" It would not have occurred to me to blame my philosophy, that I hadn't set my sail correctly.

It would not have occurred to me to say, "Well, I got this lousy philosophy and that's why I only have pennies in my pocket and nothing in the bank and things aren't working well." No. I found it much easier to blame the government, much easier to blame taxes. I used to say taxes are too high. The top tax rate when I first started paying taxes was 91 percent. So I said that was way too high. Now the top income tax rate is about 37 percent, but people are still saying taxes are too high.

I used to blame my circumstances—the company I worked for didn't pay enough, the company policies were too harsh, I'd blame the traffic, the weather, anything that came to mind. People say, "I'm too tall, I'm too short, I'm too old. I was raised in obscurity, raised on a farm, my parents were of modest means," and such. It's so easy to blame our circumstances for what's wrong with our lot in life.

So, I figured that my future was going to be tied to whatever everybody else was arranging, the economy and interest rates, etc. I used to say things cost too much. That was my whole explanation for my life at the time.

Then my teacher, my mentor taught me better. He said I needed to define my own personal philosophy. Each person's personal philosophy is exciting because it makes us different from plants and trees and dogs and birds and cats and spiders and alligators. That's what makes us different from all life forms. The ability to think, the ability to use our mind, the ability to process ideas and not just operate by instinct.

When winter approaches, the goose can only fly south. What if south doesn't look too good? Tough luck. It can only fly south. Human beings are not like a goose that can only fly south. You can turn around, go north, you can go east, you can go west. You can order the entire process of your own life, and you do that by the way you think.

We do that by exercising our mind. We do that by processing ideas and coming up with a better philosophy, a better strategy and plans for our life and goals for the future. All this comes from developing our philosophy. Philosophy helps us process what's available.

How do you turn what's available into equity and promise and lifestyle and dreams and future? You consider all the possibilities. Start with what is the seed? What is the soil? What is the sunshine? What is the rain? Is it possible to take some of each of all that's available and turn it into food and turn it into value and turn it into nourishment, turn it into something spectacular and unique that no other life form can do? The answer is yes. But you can't deal with all this and what to do with it unless you define and then refine your philosophy. Think, use your mind, come up with ideas, and strengthen your philosophy.

Keeping with our nature analogy, the seed and the soil and the rain and the sunshine are called the economy, and the banks and the money and the schools and everything that's available is what we process as information—deciding what to do with all that and turn it into equity and value. That is the major challenge of life—my personal opinion.

So, each person's personal philosophy determines what they will do with the seed and soil and sunshine and rain and the miracle, the change of seasons. Your personal philosophy is setting your sail to travel through life with a determined-by-you destiny.

TRIM A BETTER SAIL

That's what this book is all about—to help you adjust your sail to use the wind's power to propel you forward in life. You don't need a better economy. You don't need better seed and soil. In fact, when it comes to seed and soil and rain and sunshine and seasons and the miracle of life, that's actually all you have.

Don't blame what you have. If you blame the economy and you blame the schools and you blame the teachers and you blame the sermons and the preachers and you blame the marketplace and you blame the company and company pol-icy, what else is there? When some people get through with their blame list, there's nothing else. That's all there is—life becomes dormant.

Blaming the only things you have to work with is a colossal mistake. You can't say, "I'll take three springs, four summers, nine falls, and no winters." No, life doesn't work that way. You have to take it as it comes. So what do you change to make your life for the better? You start with your philosophy, your outlook, your view of life.

To change my own future, I had to change my mind. I had to change my thinking. I had to change my philosophy. I was messed up and confused about what was causing my stagnant-life problem. As soon as I stopped blaming the government and taxes, the marketplace, the economy, neg-ative relatives, and cynical neighbors and focused on the real problem—*me*—my life exploded into positive and exciting changes.

My bank account changed immediately; my income changed immediately. My whole life took on an entirely new look and color immediately—and the early results I received from making these philosophical changes tasted so good I've never stopped the process from that day until this.

And I'm telling you, with a little consideration to refine your direction by setting a better sail and refining your philosophy, your whole life can start to change starting today. You don't have to wait till tomorrow. You don't have to wait till next month. You don't have to wait till spring. You can start this whole process immediately. I recommend it.

Some people do so little thinking, they don't even have their sail up. You can imagine where they're going to wind up at the end of this week, at the end of this month, at the end of this year—wherever the tide tows them. Now, today, is your chance, your opportunity to change your thought process and absorb all this information to enhance your life. So number one is philosophy—set your mind and thinking on navigating your future toward success.

FAILURE AND SUCCESS

First, let's define success and failure.

Failure is a few errors in judgment repeated every day.

I use the example of my dad and his midnight snack. Before going to bed he has an apple, a few graham crackers, and a glass of grapefruit juice. No wonder he was healthy enough not to retire even at 88 years old. My mom taught Dad and I good health practices, and I'm fortunate enough to say I haven't been ill for many decades. Our two grown daughters and grandchildren have never been ill. Mom's guidance and Dad's legacy lingers on.

The phrase has been said for generations, "An apple a day keeps the doctor away." What if that's true?

You may say, "Well, Mr. Rohn, if that's true, that would be easy to do." Yet, if you think it's easy, then what's the problem? Why don't more people eat an apple a day to stay healthy?

Answer: It's not easy. It's easy not to adopt a good habit as your own personal philosophy. How about the person on television who tells you that a Hershey bar a day will make your day better? Your philosophy has to be stronger and smarter than to fall for the ploy that a Hershey bar a day is healthier than an apple a day. If you make that kind of error in judgment every day for six years, it will accumulate into disaster.

At first you may say, "Well, I'm very healthy now, so what difference is candy once a day rather than fruit once a day going to make?" Just because disaster doesn't fall on us at the end of the first day doesn't mean disaster isn't coming. You have to look down the road, past today, and ask, "What will the errors in my present judgment cost me in one month or six months, one year, six years?" I'm telling you right now, the money cost and health cost and success cost is too gigantic to even calculate.

This apple-a-day is a good illustration of what errors in judgment lead to—which is where I found myself at age 25.

I started working when I was 19, and met my teacher who helped turn my life around when I was 25. That's six years. At the end of the first six years of my economic life, I had pennies in my pocket, nothing in the bank.

My personal philosophy was totally messed up—my daily errors in judgment resulted in accumulated disaster. Don't be lax about developing your personal philosophy. It doesn't matter whether it's your health or your bank account, if you don't pay attention to your health, relationships, work, finances, etc., you will fail to succeed.

Success is a few disciplines practiced every day.

The formula for success is a few simple disciplines practiced every day; do this and you'll start a whole new process to establish an entirely new life. When you decide today to go for the apple instead of the Hershey bar, you have begun the process of turning your life around. And if you continue that process, not only with your health habits but your money habits, your communication habits, your sales habits, management habits, and all your habits—if you start that process and eliminate the errors and replace them with disciplines, your life will positively change immediately.

Starting even today, you never have to be the same again—only by your choice. Where would you start? With an apple. You don't have to start with some staggering discipline. How about walking around the block for your good health? What will that do for you in six years? You *could* and you *should* but most *don't*. Here's an even stronger word—most people *won't*. *Don't* might mean you're careless. *Won't* probably means you're stubborn and both may lead you to accumulated failure.

BETTER THINKING

After I realized that I was holding myself back with my blaming philosophy, during the next six years, I became a millionaire. By the time I was 31, I was a millionaire. What happened? Well, strangely enough, during that second six years of my economic life, the government was about the same, taxes were about the same. My negative relatives were the same, the economy was about the same, prices were about the same, and everything else was about the same. Circumstances were about the same. So how did I become rich? I totally changed my life—*I* was not the same.

I started with my philosophy. I started amending my errors by doing some better thinking, changing my mind, coming up with ideas that I didn't have before I met my teacher, and once that whole process started for me, I changed my whole life. Within a six-year period, I was never the same—and I continue to work on myself, to improve.

The same thing can happen for you as a teenager, as a parent, business person, salesperson, manager, wherever you find yourself. Start with your own philosophy, which is going to determine whether or not you go for the simple daily disciplines or continue making daily errors in judgment. Each of us has it within their power to make changes.

If you change philosophy, you can become capable, powerful, sophisticated, healthy, influential, all the other equities that you could possibly want out of your life using only what there is, not blaming or trying to change what's not possible to change—weather, seasons, etc. Appreciate all of life's ups and downs, with all of its mystery of why it works and sometimes it doesn't work.

I hope I intrigued you enough to study it, to ponder it—so you will commit to eating an apple a day and or taking a daily walk around the block. If you don't start there, where else will you start? Might as well start where it's easy and then go to the more complicated discipline key, your philosophy.

RESPONSIBILITY AND SELF-RELIANCE

Take responsibility for whatever happens to you, knowing that you have consciously made the decisions that are now affecting you, knowing that what is happening now today is the direct result of your activity—what you did yesterday.

Self-reliance is basically counting on yourself. Being self-reliant doesn't mean you can't work with others or trust others. Self-reliance means being responsible to and for yourself, counting on yourself, trusting yourself, being confident with yourself, trusting your own instincts, trusting the conclusions that you have developed from your study of experiences and philosophies. Taking the credit due you. Learning from mistakes you have made.

Gestalt[1] psychologists' example of being self-reliant says that you're responsible for getting caught in the rain. By deciding not to carry an umbrella every day, you have decided to endure an occasional drenching. Translation—by not being prepared, you choose to get caught in some of life's unpleasant circumstances, be it rain, failures, economic losses, relationship losses, professional losses, personal losses. By not being prepared, thinking ahead, it's your choice.

Now the other side of self-reliance is by being prepared, you increase your chances of success, of seizing opportunities when they come your way, of being ready within yourself to take advantage of once-in-a-lifetime situations.

My approach to better my future very early on in my career was to just go through the day with my fingers crossed. I used to make comments such as, "I sure hope things will change for the better." But things were not going to change—*I* had to change. When you change, when you get better, life will get better. Don't put the blame on someone else or just hope that your life will improve.

Take personal responsibility for yourself. You can't change the circumstances or the seasons or the wind, but you can change your reading habits. You can change whether or not you improve or expand your skills. Burn the midnight oil, turn yourself around, multiply your value by two, three, five, ten times. Take charge over what you can control.

You don't control the constellations, but you have control over whether or not you attend night school. Take adult classes, learn new skills. You have control over that, and if you don't follow through knowing that it will improve your situation, that's your fault.

You have to be self-reliant. You. No one else can change your life, alter your ambitions, pave a golden road for you. It's up to *you*. Learn to reap the harvest without complaint. This is a sign of growing maturity—taking full responsibility for everything you do.

Self-preparation leads to control over your life. Whenever you prepare correctly, you're taking all the steps you're supposed to take and doing everything in your power to stay on track. Whenever your preparations lead to success, achieving your goals, you reinforce the disciplines that got you there. Success leads to reinforcement of the proper disciplines. If what you're doing is working, keep doing it. If what you're doing isn't working, change it.

POSITIVE REINFORCEMENT

When you are doing all that you can possibly do and are successful at reaching your expectations, keep doing it. Success is a reinforcement. Psychologists call this positive reinforcement. Positive reinforcement is how we train our dogs and teach our kids. You reward them when they get good grades. You teach them that the skills they are developing now will have great positive effects on their lives later, but you reward them now.

Positive reinforcement is learning that there are rewards for doing something good, something worthwhile, something of value. The better you do, the better your reward. The greater the value, the greater the reward. A bigger paycheck, a better house, financial freedom. It's all a reward system.

TWO MAJOR BENEFITS OF POSITIVE REINFORCEMENT

The first major benefit of positive reinforcement is that it builds good habits. If your habits are building your ambition and increasing your success, keep doing them. Your success is reaffirming that these habits are good. Your success tells you that you need to keep doing what you're doing. By reviewing these habits that bring on success, you reinforce them. Give them sticking power.

Now, here's the other side. By reviewing your habits, you may find that some habits are inhibiting your success. You may find that what you're doing every day is bad for you, or you may realize that you're not practicing your good habits anymore. Maybe you're not taking your daily walk around the block or eating an apple a day. Well, you may have to get in the habit of not feeling well. Maybe you got out of the habit of reading books. Well, start that habit again. Make your disciplines your daily good habits routine.

When I became a millionaire, I found it was easy. My definition of easy: something I can do. I figure if it's something you can do, it's easy; but here's a little parenthesis—I worked hard at it. I made sure my disciplines were in line. I made sure my habits were good. I made sure I did all that I could. I found something that I could do, and I worked hard at it. I got up early, stayed up late, and worked hard from age 25 to 31.

Some ask, "If it's easy, why aren't more people millionaires?" Answer: because it's easier to keep doing what doesn't work. It's easier to keep bad habits. It's easier not to develop the disciplines. It's easier not to. What is easy to do is also easy *not* to do. That's the difference between success and failure, between daydreams and ambitions.

SECOND BENEFIT OF POSITIVE REINFORCEMENT

The second benefit of positive reinforcement is that it creates the energy to fuel additional achievement. Positive reinforcement gives you the drive to do more, to not only keep doing what's right but to do more of what's right—the disciplines that help you grow and get ahead of it all. Knowing that what you're doing is paying off creates more energy to keep going.

How easy is it to get up in the morning? When you're not doing all that it takes, it's not very easy at all. You can just lay there awake thinking, *Oh, what's a few more minutes in bed? It won't matter much anyway.* Wrong. It *does* matter. It *will* matter.

But how easy is it to get up in the morning when you're pouring it on, doing the best you can, anxious to get going, make progress toward your dreams? It's a whole different story when you're resting to renew your reserves; it's much different from resting to avoid your day.

When you're psyched up and excited for your life, when you're excited for what you've planned to accomplish for the day, it's amazing. You wake up before the alarm clock even tries to startle you awake. Your successes fuel your ambition. Your successes give you extra energy. Your successes pave the way for more successes. There's a snowball effect. With one success, you're excited to meet another and another and another; and pretty soon, the disciplines that were so difficult in the beginning, the disciplines that got you going are now part of your philosophy.

How do you know when you're successful? Do you have to be a millionaire? No. All that is asked of you is to earn all you possibly can. If you earn less than $40,000 a year and that's the best you can do, that's enough. God and everything else will see to it that you're okay. The key is to just do the best you can. If it's $30,000 a year, wonderful. If it's $100,000 a year, wonderful. If it's a million a year, wonderful. It doesn't matter as long as you've done the best you possibly can and have earned the most you possibly can. And here's why—*the essence of life is growth,* to do the best you can.

It's interesting that humans are the only life form that will do less than they possibly can, that will settle for less. All life forms, except human beings, strive to their maximum capacity. How tall will a tree grow? As tall as it possibly can. Trees don't grow half way; trees send their roots down as deep as possible, stretch their limbs up as high as possible, produce every leaf possible and every fruit possible.

As a matter of fact, you never heard of a human physically growing halfway. We keep growing until we're done. That's part of life we can't control; it's genetically coded. It's the rest of our growing that we control, the growing and expansion of our minds. We can control that, and it tends to get away from us. All life forms inherently strive to their max except human beings.

Why wouldn't human beings strive to their maximum possibility? Because we've been given the dignity of *choice.*

It makes us different from alligators and trees and birds. The dignity of choice makes us different from all other life forms. So, it's our choice to become *some* of what we could be, do *just enough* to get by, or become *all* we can be.

My best advice for you is to choose the *all*. Earn all you can, make all the friends you can, read as many books as you can, develop as many skills as you can, see as much as possible. Do as much as possible, make as much fortune as possible, give as much of it away as possible. The max. There's no life like it. Once I got on track, I've never looked back. Pick up the challenge. Go for it. Take the best of the two easys. Take the route—it's easy to get ahead. It's easy to do all you can. It's easy to succeed. It's easy to have financial freedom. The more you do, the more you get.

In summary, the two primary benefits of positive reinforcement are: 1) to build good habits, and 2) to create more energy to fuel your ambitions, your desires, your achievements.

How can you isolate what's working for you and what isn't? How can you make sure that you are reinforcing your positive disciplines? If it isn't obviously apparent, you need to keep track; write it down. *Keep a journal* to make sure that what you're doing is making measurable progress.

Write down everything that may be relevant in your day—what you did, who you saw, what you felt, how it may or may not affect you now and in the future. The best way to track your activities of the day is to write them down. The best way to analyze your progress through the year is to have written it down. Why? So you can look back and review it. By keeping a written record of your life, you will be more accountable. By putting into writing the action steps that you have planned, you will easily see what works and what doesn't.

Most people just try to get through the day, never writing anything down, never keeping track of their progress along the way, never really knowing if they are doing all they can to reach their goals, to drive their ambition—but gifted people learn to write down what happens each day. They don't let a day end without picking up some valuable experience, some emotional content, some idea that may positively affect their future.

To get the most from each day, week, month, and year is to take time to reflect. How can you reflect unless you record it in history so you can look back and analyze it? How can you learn from past mistakes and bask in past successes unless you write it all down? There's something extraordinary in writing out a problem. It's almost as though when you start writing it, you start figuring out ways to make it work. Perhaps that's because when you write it down, you can be more objective. You can start to see objectively where you fit into the picture. You can start to see if you are being responsible. If you are being self-reliant, you are pondering it. You are trying to figure it all out.

The fact that the issue is now on paper actually creates a space between you and the problem; and in this space you have created, solutions have room to grow. Writing about events helps you understand exactly what is happening. When we describe life to ourselves only in our minds, our imaginations tend to feed false, distorted information about how things are. Sometimes our creativity can create scenarios that really don't exist at all if we keep the information only in our mind.

But by writing it all down, we now can become more factual, more accurate, more realistic, more logical; then as we reread what we have written, we create a new picture in our mind, and once we see things as they are rather than how we think they are, we can see our way to make them better. It's all part of being responsible.

Most people dread accepting responsibility. That's just a fact of life and we can see it in operation every day. We can see ourselves getting hot under the collar when the dentist keeps us waiting and we're sitting there reading old magazines when our appointment was 30 minutes ago—and we don't stop to think that we forgot to mail this month's mortgage payment.

We can see ourselves growing angrier and angrier because a business contact is supposed to call at noon, and here it is almost two o'clock and the phone still refuses to ring, but we don't stop to think about the calls we ourselves have forgotten to return while we've been so busy fuming. We can see ourselves writing an angry letter to the airline because a flight was delayed, but we don't write an angry letter to ourselves when we're late for something, even though that might not be a bad idea at all.

Yes, we can see avoidance of responsibility all the time in both our personal and professional lives, and here's something else we can see just as often—we can see that most people aren't as successful as they wish they were. Do you see there's a connection between these two very common phenomena? I certainly do. I hope you'll understand that it's in your best interests to take responsibility for everything you do, but that's only the beginning.

There are people in their 30s and 40s who still act like adolescents, and people in their 40s and 50s who still act like babies as far as their attitude toward responsibility. People who shirk responsibility can also provide opportunities for you—if you are determined to be different. If you decide to be one of the few who embraces responsibility, you can lead and you will deserve to lead. Winston Churchill said, "The price of greatness is responsibility," and in my opinion, it's a rather small price to pay.

Regardless of negative influences in your life, the best thing you can do, the most empowering, the strongest, and ultimately the wisest course of action is to accept responsibility for your own destiny. Plain and simple. The benefits of this approach have been proven in dramatic ways. People afflicted by serious illness, for example, appear to have a better chance of recovery if they take responsibility for the situation rather than seeing themselves as victims of fate.

Take, for instance, the man who for years gained more and more weight from an unhealthy eating habits. Then he was diagnosed with severe diabetes. The physicians assured him that the disease was as much due to heredity as to unhealthy behavioral patterns. But because he was a man of strong character, in the face of this new challenge, he resolved to take responsibility for his own well-being. He saw himself as the cause of what happened; not only in his own life, but in the lives of his family and others.

The doctors told him his diabetes might have come on even if he hadn't been overeating and overworking, but he knew that was nonsense. "Baloney." He said, "It's all my fault and I'm going to do something about it. In fact, I'm going to do a lot about it." He radically changed his diet and his lifestyle. He is now in significantly better physical shape, is entering his final year of law school, and is negotiating with several companies to market his behavioral science techniques for reversing juvenile obesity.

Anybody can have an excuse for absolutely anything, and people have never been better at it than they are today. But the downside of excuses, even good ones, is that nobody really believes them. I don't care what people tell you. If you make excuses, they're going to know it and they're going to think less of you, but if you refuse to rely on excuses, people are going to know that too, and they'll admire you for it. This is especially true in business.

One of the classic examples happened in 1982:

> In 1982, Extra Strength TYLENOL® capsules in Chicago pharmacies were laced with cyanide, resulting in the death of seven people. Johnson & Johnson responded to the tampering incidents with immediacy—issuing a mass recall of 31 million bottles. The company developed an industry-leading triple tamper-evident seal, and then returned the popular product to the market. Because of Johnson & Johnson's policy of transparency and its effective response to the incidents, the product quickly rebounded to its former strength.[2]

If the company had not taken immediate action, there may have been more deaths and there would've been a tremendous loss of confidence from consumers and employees. Although unknown person(s) committed the criminal act, nevertheless, the company took responsibility for what had been done to their product, immediately remedied the situation, and took additional precautions against future possibilities. Consequently, the public image of the company was restored.

A successful person not only must accept, but eagerly desires to accept responsibility. It means making a conscious decision to grow up, to let go of the dependency needs of childhood and adolescence, and recreate yourself as somebody other people can depend on.

If you want to be a leader, if you want to enjoy a successful future, you must choose to assume responsibility for whatever happens whether you have to or not. It's like being at the helm of a ship. You are responsible for everything that takes place on your watch. You must trim your sails to move you forward toward doing what is best for all involved. Your life and how it turns out is ultimately up to you.

NOTES

1. "Gestalt psychology is a school of thought that seeks to understand how the human brain perceives experiences as whole, rather than as sums of parts." Nathalia Bustamante, "What Is Gestalt Psychology?" *SimplyPsychology,* September 7, 2023; https://www.simplypsychology.org/what-is-gestalt-psychology.html; accessed July 12, 2024.

2. "Tylenol Tampering Incidents and Recall, 1982"; Johnson&Johnson; https://ourstory.jnj.com/tylenol%C2%AE-tampering-incidents-and -recall; accessed July 13, 2024.

2

SETTING YOUR GOALS

Of all the things that changed my life for the better most quickly, it was learning how to set goals—and mastering this unique process can have a powerful effect on your life too.

One morning at breakfast, shortly after I met Mr. Shoaff, a very wealthy man who became my mentor, he asked me if he could see my current list of goals. He said, "Let me see your list of goals and let's go over them and talk about them. Maybe that's the best way I can help you right now."

I said, "I don't have a list."

He said, "Well, young man, that's where we better start. If you don't have a list of your goals, I can guess your bank balance within a few hundred dollars." Which he did, and that got my attention.

I asked, "You mean if I had a list of goals, that would change my bank balance?"

He answered, "Drastically."

That day I became a student of how to set goals; and sure enough, when I learned how to do that, my whole life changed—my income, my bank account, my personality, my lifestyle, and my accomplishments. So now I share with you the best I have learned and used successfully throughout my life.

GOAL SETTING

First of all, we are all affected by five factors:

1. Environment—family, social, career, etc.

2. Events—marriage, deaths, relocations, etc.

3. Knowledge—education or lack of, etc.

4. Results—successes and failures in various aspects of everyday life

5. Dreams—often overlooked yet affect our lives and our view of the futureWe will get into all of these influences, but here let me concentrate on the fifth one, dreams. Of all these five influences, I urge you to make your dreams the greatest influence on your daily decisions and activities.

Put another way, *make sure that the greatest pull on you is the pull of the future.* For your dreams to greatly influence you for the future, to pull you, your future must be well planned.

There are two ways to face the future—one is with *apprehension,* the other with *anticipation.* Guess how many people face the future with apprehension? Too many. They don't have their future well-designed; and without really thinking about it, they have probably bought someone else's view of how to live.

You will face the future with *anticipation* when you have planned a future you can get excited about, when you have designed your future results in advance. In this way, the future will capture your imagination and exert an enormous positive influence on you.

To design your future, you must have goals. Well-defined goals are like a magnet. They pull you in the right direction— and the better defined, the better you have described them, the harder you work on them, the stronger they pull you to great accomplishments. They also will pull you through all kinds of difficulties too.

You can either make a living or design a life.

Without goals, it's easy to let life deteriorate to the point where you're just making a living. It's not difficult to get trapped by economic necessity and settle for existence rather than substance. We all have a choice. We can either make a living or design a life.

Mr. Shoaff said to me, "I don't think your current bank balance is a true indicator of your level of intelligence." I was happy to hear that. He said, "I think you have plenty of talent and ability and that you're much smarter than your bank balance indicates." And that turned out to be true. I was much smarter.

My question to him, "Then why isn't my bank balance bigger?"

"You don't have enough reasons for accomplishing great things. If you had enough reasons, you could do incredible things. You have enough intelligence but not enough reasons. That's the key. If you had enough reasons."

In my years of study, I've discovered his answer to be true. Reasons come first and answers come second. Life has a strange way of hiding all the answers and disclosing them only to people who have been inspired to look for them, who have reasons to look for them. Put another way, *when you know what you want and you want it badly enough, you will find ways to get it.* The answers, the methods, the solutions will become evident to you.

What if you *had* to be rich? Are there books and other resources on the subject? The answer is yes. There are plenty of good ones; but if you don't *have* to be rich, you probably won't do the research. What drives us to find the answers is necessity, so work on your reasons first, answers second.

REASONS TO DO WELL

What are some reasons for doing well? Of course, each varies from person to person. I'm sure that if you did a little soul-searching, you could come up with a fairly strong list of reasons why you want to accomplish great things. There are personal reasons, sometimes uniquely personal reasons. Some people do well for the recognition. Some do well because of the way it makes them feel. They love the feeling of being a winner. That's one of the best reasons. I have some millionaire friends who keep working 10 to 12 hours a day making more millions, and it's not because they need the money. It's because of the joy, pleasure, and satisfaction that come to them from being constant winners. To them, money is not their main drive. It's the journey.

Once in a while, someone says to me, "If I had a million dollars, I'd never work another day in my life." Hey, that's probably why the good Lord sees to it that he doesn't get his million—because he'd just quit.

Family is another reason or motivator for doing well. Some people do extremely well because of other people, and that's a powerful reason. Sometimes we will do things for someone else that we would not do for ourselves. We are made that way. I met a man who said to me, "Mr. Rohn, to do everything I want to do around the world with my family, I need at least a quarter of a million dollars a year." I thought, *Incredible. Could a man's family affect him that much?* And the answer is, of course.

How fortunate are the people who find themselves greatly affected by someone else? Very fortunate—it's powerful. Benevolence is the desire to share and can be a strong motivating reason for wanting to achieve. Some people do extremely well, gathering up resources so they can then be benefactors.

When the hugely successful and wealthy steel magnet Andrew Carnegie died, in one of the desk drawers was found a slip of paper. On that slip of paper Mr. Carnegie had written his goal for his life; he wrote it when he was in his 20s. He had written, *I'm going to spend the first half of my life accumulating money. I'm going to spend the last half of my life giving it all away.* That's terrific. He was so inspired by that goal that during the first half of his life he accumulated $450 million, and during the last half of his life he gave it all away. How powerful! His giving still affects millions of people worldwide today.

What turns you on? What gets you up early, hitting it hard all day and staying up late? What inspires you? Next question, what turns you off? When I found the answers to those questions, my life exploded into change. I finally realized that my negative philosophy of life limited me, had turned me off from becoming all I could be. I cured that!

Then I found a long enough list of reasons to turn me on; and once the lights went on for me at age 25, they have never gone out. I've fallen out of the sky a few times, but I've never lost that drive to do something unique with my life.

DECIDE, CHOOSE

Goal-setting is not mysterious. Here's how simple goal setting is: Decide what you want and write it down. Write a list and answer these questions:

- Where do you want to go?
- What do you want to do?
- What do you want to see?
- What do you want to be?

- What do you want to have?

- What do you want to share?

- What projects would you like to support?

- What would you like to be known for?

- What skills would you like to learn?

- What are some extraordinary things you'd like to do?

- What are some ordinary things you'd like to do?

- Silly little things you'd like to do?

- Very important things you'd like to do?

Decide. Make decisions and choices on all those topics and whatever else comes to your mind—and write down your answers. Write it all down. That's how simple it is.

It's your own private list, so be honest. If you think it may fall into unfriendly hands, write it in code so no one else can understand it.

There's a story I tell in most of my seminars and cite in books because it's a great example about how your list will motivate you toward a successful future: I had written a little revenge on my first list. A finance company used to harass me because I was two or three payments behind. One guy called incessantly, putting me down something fierce. It was embarrassing to say the least.

When I met Mr. Shoaff and straightened out my life, one of the first things on one of my lists was to go to pay off the finance company. I needed a little drama in my life, so when I finally got the money to pay the debt, I put it all in small bills in a big briefcase, and walked into the office on Wilshire Boulevard in Los Angeles. I opened the door to the guy's office who so unkindly harassed me, walked up to his desk, and stood right in front of him.

He said, "What are you doing here?" I didn't say a word. I opened the briefcase, dumped the pile of money on his desk and said, "Count it. It's all there. I'll never be back." I turned around, walked out, slammed the door. Now that might not be very noble, but it sure felt good. Pay off with a little drama— you'll enjoy it too. It felt even better to check that debt off my list. Keep your list with you.

I keep my goals list in my journal so I can go back to previous years and compare. For instance, when I go back five years, I'm a little embarrassed at what I thought was so important. I can see how my philosophy has changed from ten years ago, five years ago, three years ago, and how my current goals compare. The lists reveal what was valuable then and now.

I can keep moving forward to each goal by identifying what I want my life to be now, where I want to go, what I want to do, what I want to see. Keep your list of goals to show your growth, your ability to change and improve. Your philosophy grows and expands what's valuable. It doesn't matter how small or foolish you think it may be; put it on your list.

Setting goals is profound, a life-changing process. But it's not hard. Just decide what you want and write it down. Get together with your spouse, decide. Get together with your kids, decide. Get together with your business colleagues, decide. Write it down. Make a list. That's how easy it is.

A MILLIONAIRE MINDSET

Here's another scenario on setting goals. When I started making my first list, Mr. Shoaff said, "Mr. Rohn, looks like we're going to be together for a while, so I have a suggestion for you. You're 25 years old. Sure, you've made some mistakes, but now you're on the road to better things. You have a family, so you have every reason to do this. Why don't you, among all the goals you're going to set, why don't you set a goal to become a millionaire? A millionaire. This is America. All the possibilities are available. Why don't you set a goal to become a millionaire? It's got a nice ring to it. Enough zeros to impress your accountant. And here's why."

I'm thinking, *Of course I know why, it would be great to have a million dollars!* As if reading my mind, he said, "No, that's not it. Here's why." And what followed was one of the greatest lessons I ever learned and I'm about to share it with you. If you can capture what I'm about to share with you, your life will change for the better.

Mr. Shoaff said, "Set a goal to become a millionaire—*for what it will make of you to achieve it.*"

That was the greatest life lesson I ever learned in one sentence. Set a goal that'll make you stretch for what it will make of you to achieve it. What a brand-new reason for setting goals! What an all-encompassing challenge to have a better vision of the future! What for? To see what it will make of you to achieve it. And here's why—the greatest value in life is not what you get. *The greatest value in life is what you become.*

The major question to ask yourself about your job is not, *What am I getting here?* The major question to ask is, *What*

The greatest value in life **is what you become.**

am I becoming here? It's not what you get that makes you valuable. It's what you become that makes you valuable.

The key phrase to remember about setting goals—*set the kind of goals that will make something of you to achieve them.* Always keep that in mind. *What will this goal make of me? If I set this goal and go for it, not only will I achieve it, but what will it make of me in the process?* What a whole new and important concept on setting goals!

TWO PARTS TO GOAL SETTING

There are two parts to goal setting: 1) don't set your goals too low and 2) don't compromise.

NUMBER ONE, DON'T SET YOUR GOALS TOO LOW.

A lesson we teach in leadership seminars: Don't join an easy crowd, you won't grow. Go where the expectations are high. Go where the demands are high. Go where the pressure is on to perform, to grow, to change, to develop, to read, to study, to develop skills.

I belong to a small group. We do business around the world. You cannot believe the expectations at that level. What we expect of each other in terms of excellence is far beyond average. Why? So we can each grow, so we can receive from the group, we can contribute to the group something unprecedented. It's called living at the summit. Go where the demands are high. Go where the expectations are strong to provoke you, push you, urgently insist that you not remain the

Set the kind of goals that will make something of you to achieve them.

same for the next couple of years, the five years that you'll grow and change. So don't set your goals too low. Someone says, "Well, I don't need much." Well, then you don't need to become much.

NUMBER TWO, DON'T COMPROMISE, DON'T SELL OUT.

There were some things I went for back in those early years that if I had known how much it was going to cost me, I never would've paid, but I didn't know. Always count the cost. You may be familiar with an ancient story that says Judas got money for being a traitor—and he was so unhappy that he committed suicide.

The greatest source of unhappiness is self-unhappiness, which comes from inside, where the erosion starts. That's where the beginning little infection of unhappiness starts—doing a little less than you can, not feeling good about yourself. Don't let that happen. An ancient script sums it all up, "What if you gain the whole world but it costs you your soul?" Don't compromise your values. Don't compromise your virtues. Don't compromise your philosophy. Beware of the cost.

Mark well what you become in pursuit of what you want. I'm inspiring you to set the kinds of goals to transform your life and make you far better than you are, far stronger than you are.

POSITIVE SELF-DIRECTION

You know who you are and where you want to go. You've already spent a great deal of time thinking about it. You've been working on the parts of your personality that will make you better. Working on your attitude, working on your health, working on your time management skills, putting it all down on paper. You constantly see yourself in the place where you want to be.

As you talk with yourself every day, how often do you ask, *Is what I'm doing today getting me closer to where I want to be tomorrow? Am I making the daily adjustments necessary? Am I doing all that it takes? Will I keep on doing it until...?* Direction determines destination. Here are two more questions you need to ask yourself: Are all of the disciplines that I'm currently engaged in taking me where I want to go? Are all of the disciplines I'm presently engaged in taking me where I want to go?

These are important questions to ask yourself at the beginning of the month, at the beginning of the week, at the beginning of the day—because you never want to kid yourself. Kid your neighbor and kid me and kid the marketplace if you want to, but you can't kid yourself with your fingers crossed, hoping you'll arrive at a good destination when you're not even headed that way.

You say, "Well, maybe the wind will take me there." Perhaps a slim chance. Rather, you have to take charge. You have to ask yourself often, *Am I doing what I need to do to take me in the direction I want to go?* Don't be faked out thinking you're on the way to financial success when you're not putting in the time and effort. Don't be faked out hoping someone else is going to take care of it, take care of you. They're not going to take care of it. And they're not going to take care of you.

WHAT IF
AND NOT MUCH

What if all of your negative relatives turned positive? What'll that do for your fortune and your future? Not much. If prices come down a little, what'll that do for your fortune and your future and your sophistication and your culture? Not much. If the economy gets a little better, what'll that do? Answer, not much. If you don't make plans of your own, you'll fit into someone else's plans, and guess what they have planned for you? You're right—not much.

Most people wake up every morning counting on this "not much" list, and that's why what they have is not much. Not much hope, not much promise, not much progress. They're driving what they don't want to drive, living where they don't want to live, doing what they don't want to do.

Forget the thief waiting in the alley to snatch your wallet. What about the thief in your mind? Lazy, not stimulated by thoughts and questions. Don't become a victim of yourself. Ask yourself these questions: Is this the direction I want for my life? Is it someone else's direction? Is it a goal I have been ingrained with since my childhood? Is it my parents' or my spouse's or my boss's or my children's? Is it my goal?

Ask yourself these questions. Debate them if you will. Debate the ideas I'm sharing with you. After you've heard all the ideas, debate what will work for you and won't work for you; but most importantly, get into the debate of your inner mind. *What am I doing that works? What am I doing that doesn't work?* Debate it all. Work with your mind to figure out the best possible direction for you.

GOALS UNIQUELY YOURS

You hear stories all the time of good kids who are having problems. Their parents are highly successful. They want their kids to be highly successful, but the kids are having problems, maybe not with their grades, but with how they feel about themselves. The parents push their kids into one career direction, probably to take over the family business or follow in the family footsteps. Those are the parents' directions, not the kid's direction. The kids know that something is just not right, and for these kids something goes wrong.

I have a friend who came from a medical family. The parents were in medicine and all the kids grew up and became doctors. It wasn't a bad upbringing. They had everything they needed, but they also had the extra push to go into medicine. She was raised with such tunnel vision that she didn't even have the slightest idea how food got into the grocery store, how cars got into the lots, how money got into the banks. These types of issues were never brought up at the dinner table.

She remembers the first time she went to look for a job to make extra money in college. The best jobs in the paper for qualified people were advertising a monthly salary of $900 (back in the 1970s). She thought the average nonqualified person made at least $3,000 a month. What a difference, what a shock.

She wondered if she was that far off in her judgment of average earnings, maybe she was way off on other thoughts about life too. Maybe there was more to life than the medical field. Even though she was chastised by her family for not following through with the family goals, she is now much happier following her own path. Direction must be your own or it can be damaging—damaging to your soul, damaging to your spirit, damaging to your health. Trimming your sail to head in the right direction has to be your own or it can be damaging.

So parents, be watchful about how you motivate your children. Give them all the resources to make their own choices and back them up. Give them the freedom to discover their own direction. It may not be the direction you hoped for, but it is their direction. And with their own direction, they will reach their own destination. It just doesn't work out any other way.

LIFE'S DIRECTION

If you had the revelation that the life and goals you're pursuing are not your own, you can make changes like my friend did, but the change doesn't come overnight. The direction of life can come overnight. A new goal can reach out and grab you in one day, give you the push and the ambition and the momentum to change your course, where you want to be. But the final destination does not happen overnight; it takes a lot of work. It still takes time for the plans to build, to grow, to run the course. It takes patience.

Let's say you have a brilliant idea for starting a new company. What's the first thing you do? You write a business plan and a marketing plan and complete the financial proformas. You don't expect to have an idea one day and a prospering business the next. No, it doesn't work that way. You have to take all the right steps, give it care and nurturing and time, lots of time for your investment to start reaping rewards. You have to be patient. But here's what does happen. As soon as you turn a new direction, you have an excellent chance of journeying toward a brand-new destination.

GOALS ACCOMPLISHED

Keep track on your list of the goals you accomplish. It's very important when you reach a goal to celebrate that milestone. Celebrate every significant and important-to-you accomplishment. It doesn't have to be world-changing or life-changing. If it's just a goal that's important to you and you finally reached it, celebrate. Hopefully on your list of goals you had some family goals, and if the family together reaches a goal, celebrate together. Celebration creates excitement to develop a longer list.

You also need ongoing goals. When the early astronauts went to the moon, some when they returned to Earth had psychological problems. Some drank too much and got into other difficulties. One of the reasons why this happened is because they accomplished an amazing feat—and where do you go from there? Later, those in charge made sure that the astronauts who came back from the moon had plenty of projects to keep them busy. The same is true of you and me— make new goals after you've reached the ones on your list, then make another list, and so on.

So, keep making new goals to replace goals that you've achieved—for the rest of your life. How far should you go? As far as you can. How many books should you read? As many as you can.

How many friends should you make? As many as you can. How much should you earn? As much as you can. You should try to be all you possibly can be. Stretch yourself, think, wonder, ponder. *I wonder what might be possible. If I could get everything I wanted, what would that be?*

As mentioned at the beginning of this chapter, goal-setting is not hard or mysterious—just decide what you want and write it down. If you didn't already, take time now to answer these questions:

- Where do you want to go?

  _____

- What do you want to do?

  _____

- What do you want to see?

  _____

- What do you want to be?

  _____

- What do you want to have?

  _____

- What do you want to share?

  _____

- What projects would you like to support?

  _____

- What would you like to be known for?

  _____

- What skills would you like to learn?

  _____

- What are some extraordinary things you'd like to do?

  _____

- What are some ordinary things you'd like to do?

  _____

- Silly little things you'd like to do?

  _____

- Very important things you'd like to do?

  _____

- Anything else that comes to mind

  _____

  _____

  _____

  _____

WORKSHOP EXERCISE

Write four one-year goals—goals from your list that you can accomplish in one year. This is what turned me on at age 25, accomplishing goals and personal progress within the coming year. Once the fires were lit for me, I'm telling you, they have never gone out. Since I was 25 years old, no one has ever asked me, "When are you going to get going? When are you going to get off the couch? When are you going to get started?" But what I have heard is, "When are you going to slow down? You can't visit that many countries. You're going to have a heart attack and die." Amazing.

I can't say it strongly enough. It's easy to get lazy in designing the day and designing the year and designing the future and designing what you want to accomplish and just cross your fingers and hope it'll all work out, that the favorable winds will blow it all your way. I'm telling you, it's not going to happen.

THE WHY

After you have identified your four one-year goals, then ask yourself, *Why are these four goals important to me?* The *why* is very important. I'll give you some notes on that a little bit later, but right now write five or six brief sentences why those particular four goals are at the top of your one-year list.

When the *why* gets stronger, the *how* gets easier. When the *why* gets big and powerful, the *how* seems to be so much easier. Without a strong enough why, the how seems almost too difficult accomplish. When you have a strong and powerful goal, you'll figure out how to manage your time so you can plan your strategy to accomplish your goal. When your why is strong enough, you realize that the time and effort are worth it. If it's not worth it, why would you bother managing your time if it really doesn't matter?

When the why of reaching your goals really matters, you can do anything. You can get up any hour, read any book, take any class, make any change, develop any skill, do any discipline. You can do it all. When the why starts to grow, the how gets simple.

Maybe one of your goals was to have a million-dollar home on a hill overlooking a beautiful valley, mountain, or ocean scene. That would be a good goal. A million-dollar home. Here's the next question—a home for what? A house is a house is a house with wood and walls and roof. A million-dollar home would be wonderful, but what for? What purpose would it serve?

Underline this: *Purpose is stronger than object.* The object would be the house and that'll pull you toward your goal. That's a worthy goal to go for—the object is the house. But there's a stronger goal, the *purpose* for the million-dollar home. You may say, "The house will be the centerpiece of all our family's activity. A variety of people will be coming and going, and influence and interesting events will happen in this place." Now we're getting somewhere. If you understand that the purpose of your goals is what matters most, you've hit on one of my best teachings in the whole book.

Your goal's purpose is what matters most.

It's okay to have plenty of objects to go for on your goal list, but always keep asking yourself the question and sometimes it's good to write it out. Here's *why* I want this money. Here's *why* I want this place. Here's why, and you start developing good reasons, which starts to become incredibly powerful steps toward reading your goals.

PERSONAL DEVELOPMENT

Some of your goals should be *personal development, the person you wish to become.* Develop skills that make you attractive to the marketplace. *Develop the temperament and the attitude* that makes you attractive to the business world, the attitude and the temperament that makes you a splendid spouse and parent, study the art of becoming the person you were meant to be.

As mentioned previously, it's not what you *get* that makes you valuable, it's what you *become* that makes you valuable. I admired my friend Mark Hughes for the fortune he made and the company he built. Guess what I admired more? The person he became in a short 44 years. He was unique. He bought the idea at age 19 of personal development and worked on it daily from that day until the time he died.

The idea of becoming an attractive person, a skillful person, a good friend, a good colleague, a good partner, a good member of the round table, a contributor—that's the key, the person you become.

I'm telling you, these concepts and advice and examples changed my life, altered the course of my life from milking cows to presenting in front of thousands. Incredible. What a journey.

For the next exercise, I want you to look at the whole list you've written and your exercises. Now, answer this question, "What kind of person must I become to achieve all I want?"

Take your time and write down your answer. *What kind of person must I become to achieve all I want?*

_____

_____

_____

_____

_____

Now you have two things working for you: 1) what you become helps you achieve, and 2) what you achieve helps you become. The more you become, the more you can achieve, and the more you achieve, the more you can become. Who knows which affects the other the most.

WORKSHOP EXERCISE

The next exercise is to write a few sentences stating your concept of the person you think you must become to achieve what you want. It's time for truth here. Maybe you need to become wiser than you are at the moment. You may need to develop a stronger personality. You may need to adhere to a healthier lifestyle. Maybe you need a little coaching.

You may write something such as, "To be the person I want to become, I need to be coached—physical coaching, spiritual coaching, developing skills coaching, etc. To be the influence I want to be, I have to build an incredible reputation. What kind of person must I be to attract all that I want in my life and the people I want and the opportunities that I want?"

_____

_____

_____

_____

_____

3

PRINCIPLED DISCIPLINE, PROCRASTINATION, PATIENCE

Consistent and principled self-discipline is a significant key to your future success. What's at the core of achieving the good life? It's not in learning how to set goals, or how to better manage your time, or mastering the attributes of leadership. Every day in a thousand different ways we try to improve ourselves by learning how to do things. Principled discipline is acting in accordance with morality, ethics, honesty, and recognizing right and wrong.

We spend a lifetime gathering knowledge in classrooms, textbooks, and experiences. Now, if knowledge is power and the forerunner to success, then why do we fall short of our objectives? Why in spite of all our knowledge and in spite of our collective experiences do we find ourselves aimlessly wandering, settling for a life of existence rather than a life of substance?

There may be many answers to this question. Your answers may be different from your associates or your spouse or your friends. But the fundamental answer is the absence of discipline. *Applying* all that we know is principled discipline—consistent self-discipline.

It doesn't really matter how smart you are or how much you know if you don't use it. It takes consistent self-discipline to master the art of setting goals, to master the art of time management, to master the art of leadership, to master the art of parenting and relationships. If we don't make consistent self-discipline part of our daily lives, the results we seek will be sporadic and elusive.

Consistent self-discipline is vital in navigating toward your future success.

It takes a consistent effort to truly manage our valuable time or we'll be consistently frustrated. Our time will be eaten up by others whose demands are stronger than our own. It takes discipline to conquer the nagging voices in our minds, the fear of failure, the fear of success, the fear of poverty, the fear of a broken heart.

It takes discipline to keep trying when that nagging voice within us brings up the possibility of failure. It takes discipline to admit our errors and recognize our limitations. The voice of the human ego speaks to all of us. Sometimes it says that we should magnify our value beyond our results. It leads us to exaggerate, to not be totally honest. It takes discipline to be totally honest, both with ourselves and with others.

Be certain of one thing, every exaggeration of the truth once detected by others destroys our credibility and makes all that we say and do suspect. As soon as a business colleague figures out that we tend to exaggerate, guess what? They will assume that we always exaggerate and will never hold us in the same regard again, never.

The tendency to exaggerate, distort, or even withhold the truth is an inherent part of all humans.

It starts when we're kids. Johnny says, "I didn't do it. I didn't do it." Well, maybe Johnny didn't do it, but he probably had something to do with it. And this tendency continues into adulthood. Exaggerating the benefits of a product to make a sale, exaggerating our net worth to impress friends, exaggerating how close we are to closing a deal to impress the boss. Only an all-out disciplined assault can overcome this tendency.

It takes principled discipline to change a habit, because habits are formed a little bit each day, every day, every day. Once habits are formed, they act like a giant cable, like a nearly unbreakable instinct that only long-term, disciplined activity can change. We must unweave every strand of the cable of habits slowly and methodically until the cable that once held us in bondage becomes nothing more than scattered strands of wire.

It takes consistent self-discipline to:

- Plan—execute your plan, look with full objectivity at the results, and change either your plan or your method if the results are poor.
- Be firm when the world throws opinions at your feet.
- Ponder the value of someone else's opinion when your pride leads you to believe that you are the only one with the answers.

With consistent discipline applied to every area of our lives, we can discover untold miracles and uncover unique possibilities and opportunities.

What is discipline? *Discipline is a constant human awareness of the need for action and a conscious act to implement that action.* If our awareness and our implementations occur at the same time, then we begin a valued sequence of disciplined activity.

The other side of discipline? If a considerable time passes between the moment of awareness and the time of implementation, that's called *procrastination.* Procrastination is an almost exact opposite of discipline.

The voice within us says, "Get it done." Discipline then says, "Do it now." Do it to the best of your ability today, tomorrow, and always until finally, the worthy deed becomes instinctive.

Procrastination says, "I'll do it later, tomorrow, whenever I get a chance." Procrastination also says, "Do what is necessary to get by or to impress others. Do what you can but not what you must."

In every circumstance we face, we are constantly presented with these two choices: Do it now or do it later. Discipline and procrastination. A choice between a disciplined existence bearing the fruit of achievement and contentment, or procrastination. Procrastination is the easy life for which the future will bear no fruit, only the bare branches of mediocrity.

The rewards of a disciplined life are great, but they're often delayed until sometime in the future. The rewards for the lack of discipline are immediate, but minor compared to the immeasurable rewards of consistent self-discipline. *An immediate reward for lack of discipline is a fun day at the beach. A future reward of discipline is owning the beach.*

Don't choose today's pleasure for tomorrow's fortune.

Most choose today's pleasure rather than tomorrow's fortune. So how can you:

- Get rid of the easy distractions?
- Keep your mind on what you're trying to do?
- Keep an attitude of doing it all and doing it now?
- Choose discipline over procrastination?
- Stay focused on your ambitions?
- Avoid conversations at the water cooler, wasting time?

TIME MANAGEMENT DISCIPLINE

The following are keys to unlock more time in your day. Time management disciplines return many benefits:

1. Don't work harder, work smarter.

2. Take charge.

3. Reasonable time is enough time to achieve all your goals.

4. Write a set of goals and priorities.

5. Identify the critical and the routine.

6. Don't mistake movement for achievement.

7. Don't mistake courtesy for consent.

8. Concentrate.

9. Learn to say, "No."

10. Don't play at work and don't work at play.

11. Recognize your weaknesses.

12. Beware of distractions.

13. Take a step down or back.

14. Think!

15. Learn to ask questions upfront.

16. Learn to think on paper.

17. Keep track of all your appointments.

Each of these keys are explained in more detail in my book *The Day That Turns Your Life Around*.

You can do all that if you work on your consistent self-discipline on a daily basis. Never underestimate the power of your own consistent self-discipline.

Now let's take a closer look at principled discipline, at the three steps to becoming disciplined.

FIRST, TRUE DISCIPLINE IS NOT THE EASIEST OPTION.

Most people would rather sleep until 10 o'clock than get up at 6 a.m. It's easier to go to bed late, sleep late, show up late, leave early. It's easier not to read. It's easier to turn on the television than to open a book. It's easier to do just enough than to do it all. Waiting is always easier than acting. Trying is always easier than doing. Imagine what life would be like if we didn't have to make our bed in the morning or keep our garage clean or pay our taxes or show up for work tomorrow. Wouldn't it be fascinating if we didn't have to do these things? Wouldn't it be fascinating? What do you suppose would become of us? You're right, not much.

The easiest things in life are the most unprofitable.

For whatever the reason, the system we live in and contribute to is designed to make the easiest things in life the most unprofitable. Profitable seems to be the most difficult. Our world is and always will be a constant battle between the life of ease and its momentary rewards and a life of discipline and its far more significant rewards. Each has its own price—the price of discipline or the price of regret. We will pay one or the other.

What we wish we had done is the voice of regret speaking in a sorrowful tone at a time when there is no going back. This is regret. No second chance. No "What would I do differently?" Choose one or the other, but both will have their price. The price of discipline or the price of regret. One costs pennies, the other a fortune.

Dostoevsky said, "There are hundreds of young men who would die for the truth, but very few who would spend five years studying to know what the truth is." Dying for the truth is much more dramatic than the discipline of studying one little piece at a time, one day at a time, one month at a time— but in the big picture, is dying for the truth really easier than adhering to daily disciplines?

THE SECOND LESSON OF DISCIPLINE IS THAT IT'S A FULL-TIME ACTIVITY.

The best form of discipline is consistent self-discipline. The discipline that it takes to make your bed every day is the same discipline necessary for success in the world of business. The discipline to organize your garage is the same discipline to organize your business. All disciplines, good habits, carry through to affect all parts of your life. Likewise, bad habits in one area of your life will eventually destroy your self-discipline in other areas.

Standards of behavior and conduct:

- Discipline is our mind being trained to control our lives.
- Discipline is a set of standards that we've selected as a personal code of conduct.
- Discipline is imposing on ourselves the requirements for honoring these standards.

Once we've adopted these standards of behavior and conduct, we're committed to honor them. We must walk the talk. We can't act in a way far different from our beliefs. We can't tell our kids that watching television is rotting their minds, yet we spend our evenings in front of it.

We can't tell our employees they must work every minute of the working day, yet we spend three hours at lunch. "Do as I say, not as I do" is being inconsistent, which leads to a loss of credibility for others and more importantly a loss of credibility within ourselves.

The only thing worse than someone who is inconsistent in applying their self-imposed disciplines are those who never considered the need or the value of discipline. These people seem to wander aimlessly through life changing standards, procedures, loyalties, and shifting frequently from one commitment to another—leaving behind a trail of broken friendships, unfinished projects, and unfulfilled promises, all because of a discipline that was either non-existent or imposed so infrequently that it was ineffective.

NUMBER THREE SIMPLY SAYS THAT FOR EVERY DISCIPLINED EFFORT THERE ARE MULTIPLE REWARDS, WHICH IS ONE OF LIFE'S GREAT ARRANGEMENTS.

In fact, it's an extension of the biblical law that says, "If you sow well, you reap well"—which suggests that not only will we reap what we sow, we'll reap much more. Life is full of laws that both govern and explain behaviors, but this may well be the law we need to understand most. For every disciplined effort, there is a multiple reward. What a concept. If you render unique service, your reward will be multiplied.

If you're fair and honest and patient with others, your reward will be multiplied. If you give more than you expect to receive, your reward is more than you expect. But remember, the key word here is discipline. Everything of value requires care and attention.

For example, children require discipline. They must have a structure and boundaries to work within so they feel secure and comfortable to explore and grow. They must learn to recognize what's right and wrong, what's acceptable and not acceptable behavior. Children require unwavering discipline, consistent discipline, or they will be confused as to how to behave. Likewise, our thoughts require discipline. We must set up our inner boundaries, our codes of conduct, or our thoughts will be confused, producing confused results.

Look around you at this very moment in time. What might you be doing that needs attention? Perhaps you're reading while watching a mind-numbing television program. Perhaps you're reading alone because you've had a disagreement with someone you love or someone who loves you, and your anger won't allow you to speak to that person. Wouldn't this be an ideal time to examine your need for a new discipline? Perhaps you're on the brink of giving up or starting over or starting out, and the only missing ingredient to your incredible success story in the future is a new and self-imposed discipline that will make you stay longer and try harder and work more intensely than you ever thought you possibly could.

The most valuable form of discipline is the one that you impose on yourself. Don't wait for things to deteriorate so drastically that someone else must impose discipline into your life. Wouldn't that be tragic? How could you possibly explain the fact that someone else thought more of you than you thought of yourself, that they forced you to get up early and get out into the marketplace when you would've been content to let success go to someone else who cared more about themselves.

Your life, my life, the life of each one of us is going to serve as either a warning or an example. A warning of the consequences of neglect, self-pity, lack of direction and ambition—or an example of talent put to use, of discipline self-imposed, and of clearly perceived and intensely pursued objectives and goals.

Note that too much discipline can be a bad. Life without balance results in an unbalanced life. Walking around the block every day is good. Walking or running six hours a day is bad. It's obsessive unless, of course, you make your living as a marathon runner—then you're doing your job. Eating an apple a day is good. Eating only apples is bad. You won't get all the protein and vitamins and nutrients your body needs. Working hard, burning the midnight oil is good. Working nonstop, never taking a vacation, never spending quality time with the people you love is bad.

If you have your nose to the grindstone all the time, you may not spot new opportunities or make time to consider new ideas. You have to stop sometimes and ponder where you've been and where you're going—reflect so you know if you're even on the right track.

Most everyone has heard the story of Willy Loman in the play *Death of a Salesman*. Willy was a workaholic. He typified the old-fashioned concept of success. After all, if you're always working, you must be successful. No, it doesn't work that way. For workaholics there's never enough work. They can work 10, 12, 14 hours a day, take two jobs, work them back to back. The only satisfaction is fighting off sleep, denying life's pleasures, getting more tasks done. Some people are impressed with this type of behavior, but just because a workaholic spends too much time working doesn't mean he or she ends up with the most money. These people are generally more task-oriented than results-oriented.

They're busy being busy, not busy being productive. Workaholics generally end up alienating their families, losing their health, facing a crisis of values. Wouldn't you prefer a life of productivity rather than a life of tasks? Of course. When you schedule your time, you can work smarter instead of working longer, and you'll probably end up getting more done than the workaholic and still have time for other things in life.

Enlightened self-interest says, *I will look for new ways to work smarter by focusing on doing more per hour instead of doing more hours*. It says, *I will control my day so my day doesn't control me*. Enlightened self-interest also says that a life worth living comes from a life of balance and moderation. Too much of anything, even good things, will sooner or later throw you off track.

VISUAL CHAIN THINKING

There's the key technique you can use to help keep you on track called *visual chain thinking*. Ambitious people don't see each step toward their goals as a single step, each discipline as a single discipline, each project as a single project, each sale as a single sale. With everything they do and with every discipline they adhere to, they see it all as part of a chain, a link in the chain of events and actions that leads them to their final destination.

When you can see that every link in the chain eventually leads you to the things you want most out of life, to the person you want to become, you won't grow discouraged or fearful or impatient with today. When you can see where you're going through visual chain thinking, even on the toughest days, you keep building your ambition by knowing where you're going, not just where you are today.

Part of this visual chain thinking is built when you decide on your direction. When you can see where you're going to end up before you get there. When you can see California while staring at the east side of a 14,000-foot mountain. And building your visual chain of thought begins when you have well-defined plans for your career, your family activities, your investments, and your health.

Your plans and goals are your visual chain—knowing where you're going before you get there. Develop a plan, a game plan. Not one professional sports team begins a game without a complete strategy, but few of us take the time to map out a strategy for our lives, a game plan, but it's important.

YOUR LIFE'S GAME PLAN

The first rule for your game plan: *Don't start your day until you have it finished.* Don't begin your activities for the day until you know exactly what you plan to accomplish. Don't start your day until you have it planned, and do this every day. I know all that writing is time consuming and takes a disciplined effort, but remember that *value* is the fruitful result of discipline, not of *hope*.

Once you've mastered the art of planning your day, you're ready for the next level. Don't start your *week* until you have it finished. Don't begin your activities of the week until you know exactly what you plan to accomplish. Don't start your week until you have it planned. Just imagine what life would be like if you took time out of every Sunday to plan your week. Come Friday you won't be saying, "Boy, did this week fly by. Where did it go? What did I do?"

No, if you plan your week before you start it, you'll know exactly what you want to do, what you want to accomplish, what you need to work on. If you learn to plan your days as part of your overall game plan for the week, the parts will fit much better. Your days will be better, more effective. You'll be working smarter, not harder.

And when you've learned to plan your day and your week, then plan your month. Don't start your month until it's finished. By developing a game plan for your days, your weeks, and your months and following your game plan, your days, weeks, and months become part of a bigger plan, a bigger design, a long-term view of your life. A visual chain. You gain a greater perspective of it all because you are planning. It takes great discipline on your part, but it will soon lead to a new habit, a habit of mastering your time, a habit of discipline that will lead you to the good life.

Now if visually seeing the future is new to you, if you've never developed a game plan before, let me offer a few tips. There are two things that you need to understand before you create a game plan:

- Number one, a game plan, a visual chain of your future is like a spreadsheet. Instead of listing numbers, you list activities. It's like a to-do list.

- Number two, the technique of developing a game plan can be used for a single day, a single project, or a variety of projects happening simultaneously.

Here's how you do it. First of all, you need to buy a pad of graph paper. Game plans work best on graph paper. Take a sheet of graph paper and make vertical columns of the number of days this plan is to cover. Then on the left-hand side of the paper, write the heading, "Activities."

Under this heading, list all the activities to be accomplished within your timeframe. Let's say, for example, that you have one week to finalize a marketing plan. It's an overwhelming amount of work to complete, but it has to be done, so break it down piece by piece.

The best way to start is to list all the individual components on the side of the page. Now, some of these things need to be completed before others can be started. You need to have your market research results in before you can determine your target market. You need to know your target market before you can develop your marketing strategy. You need to have your marketing strategy before you can create a budget for collateral materials and so on. When you break down the project piece by piece, deadline by deadline, you can be more effective in delegating the appropriate pieces of the puzzle and you can be more effective in doing your own work while orchestrating the rest.

The final result of developing a visual chain, your game plan, is a clear visual presentation of the tasks before you.

Keep your game plan in plain sight. Put it up in your office where you can easily look at it. Have a copy of it at home and tape it to the refrigerator. Keep a copy in your journal for quick reference. Your game plan will serve as a constant reminder of all you need to do to get where you want to go.

If you're doing all that you're scheduled to do, game plans are very rewarding and the discipline of developing and following a game plan is exciting. Day by day by day, week by week by week, month by month by month, you'll see the reality of your dreams and plans come true. It's an incredible feeling of being in charge of your life, your surroundings, your future.

It's like creating a work of art on the biggest canvas imaginable. It's creative; it's beautiful. It is powerful to dream a dream, plan for the dream, and then to watch your dream turn into reality. And what's really powerful about creating game plans is that you can see your future right before your eyes. So on those days when your energy isn't up to par, your enthusiasm is a little low, your ambition isn't pulling you, and your attitude isn't on the high side—on those days use your game plan to see how far you've come and take time to realize just exactly where you're headed. On those days it's your discipline and visual chain of the future that pulls you ahead. It can't possibly set you back. It'll pull you ahead. Develop a game plan for your life and make sure that it includes more than work projects.

Make sure your game plan includes time for recreation, time for reflection, time for exercise, time for health, time for spirituality. Let's say you've developed your plan and you've penciled in writing a report from 9 a.m. to 10 a.m. Well, what if you don't do your best report writing this early in the morning? What if you do this kind of work best at 3 o'clock in the afternoon? Then juggle your projects around a little. Know yourself well enough to know what you do best at different times of the day, of the week, of the month. Know the best time for you to accomplish a certain type of task and schedule it during those times. You have to work with your game plan in order for it to best work for you—and you have to maintain consistent self-discipline to work your plan until it's completed.

In the end, it is your own discipline that acts as the catalyst to give substance and depth to your ambition. To achieve your own plans and dreams, to have what you want to have and to become what you want to become, your consistent self-discipline is the catalyst.

The ultimate question cannot be whether you are going to make the fundamental disciplines your own. The ultimate question is when are you going to focus on self-discipline? With the intense and consistent application of worthy disciplines, we have the individual and collective capacity to change ourselves, our incomes, our attitudes, our lifestyles, and our effect on other people. We can change opinions. We can change leadership. We can even change the direction of our nation. We have the capacity, we have the answers, and we have the ability. The elements are all there, including the freedom to try. Only the discipline is missing, and that element and the decision to use it lies within all of us. The choice is ours.

To maintain the momentum generated by your initial excitement about turning any area of your life around, you need to learn to master the use of your time. This involves not only the skill of time management, but the skill of time protection. In our modern world of increasing distractions,

We find ways to wait for the next paycheck, but how many can wait patiently in a checkout line in a crowded supermarket? How many people can stand and wait quietly for an overdue train or subway? It seems there are two kinds of patience—the kind that sets you up for the long term and gives you the promise of a better and richer day after tomorrow. And the other kind, the sort of patience that helps you remain sane and sociable while you're waiting in line or watching the clock.

If at all possible, greet life's little problems with calmness and patience. Because almost all problems can be solved if you take the time to see them and think them through. That's very easy to understand and it's very easy to say—but it takes strong character to put into practice.

I'm never sure what to think when people say, "I want to make a million dollars by the time I'm 40," or, "I want to retire by the age of 45." This combination of goals plus deadlines strikes me as shortsighted and maybe even a bit naïve. It takes a worthwhile goal and subjects it to an imposed time-table. You might have an idea of what a million dollars would mean to you or you might have really exciting plans for your life after you hang up your career, but I don't see how people can reasonably expect to know who or what they will be or think or feel at some arbitrary moment in the future.

This kind of thinking misses the whole point of success. The real payoff in financial and worldly success isn't the result of an amount of money divided by the age you are when you get it or some other actuarial formula. The real payoff is found in the qualities of character you develop along the way.

There's a story about a young man who had a very old and rich uncle. When the uncle died, the young man was called to the office of his attorney and told that he'd been left a huge fortune. To collect it, however, he first had to run a certain errand, which was described on a slip of paper. It seems simple enough, but when the young man tried to accomplish it, this first task turned into another and then another. As he pursued his uncle's final request, the young man was led into foreign lands and exotic adventures and untold dangers.

The real payoff are the qualities of character you develop along the way.

More years passed and the young man nearly lost track of how and even why he was on this long journey, and he could hardly imagine what its end might be. At last, the odyssey led him back into the very same lawyer's office where it had begun. "I'm here to collect my inheritance," said the heir, no longer a young man, but a much wiser one. The lawyer smiled, "As your uncle intended, you've already collected it in the places you've been and the things you've learned. And again, as he intended, it will last you for a lifetime."

Success that comes too easily or too quickly almost never lasts. For people who achieve that kind of success, there's always a lurking feeling that they haven't really earned it, and that feeling eats away at their character. If they're smart, they create some new challenge for themselves in a totally unfamiliar field. It's best to build your character to survive sudden good fortune—that's a kind of character building that kicks in during an emergency.

I think Thomas Edison put it best, "Everything comes to him who waits, but it comes sooner to him who hustles while he's waiting." There's a way of putting your best effort into something, but detaching yourself from the outcome—that's the essence of patience. It's not at all like wanting to make a certain amount of money by a certain age or winning the game before the clock runs out. The real point is to keep the clock running. The real way to win is to stay in the game for as long as it darn well takes.

4

PERSONAL GROWTH

Mr. Shoaff told me many very important success secrets including, "It's not what happens that determines the major part of your future. What happens, happens to us all; so it's not what happens. What actually determines your future is what you *do* about what happens."

He continued, saying, "If you start a process of change, you can most certainly improve your future. Start by doing something different the next 90 days than you did the last 90 days. Maybe you need to read some books, choose a new health discipline, spend more time with your family. Whatever it is, it doesn't matter how small, start changing your routine within your same circumstances. Since we can't always change the circumstances surrounding us, we can change ourselves to make the most of each day. *We can change what we think and do.*"

Then he gave me another secret to success saying, "What you have at the moment, Mr. Rohn, you've attracted by the person you've become. You don't have to change what's outside. All you have to change is what's inside. To have more, you simply have to become more. And don't wish it was easier—wish you were better. Don't wish for fewer problems—wish

What determines your future is what you do about what happens.

for more skills. Start working on yourself by making personal changes and your whole world will change for the better."

There were just a few simple principles he gave me but once I understood them, it opened my mind to so much more. I hope the same is true for you.

YOUR VALUE

The key to all good things is becoming more valuable. Why would we pay somebody $400 an hour? Because they are valuable in the marketplace for their expertise. Work hard on yourself. Make yourself more valuable to the marketplace. You can so dynamically change your income by developing your personal values, outlook, attitude, character, skills, etc.

Finances and economics are the least of the values you can start earning in terms of equity.

If you work harder on yourself than you do on your job; if you work hard on yourself and develop the skills; if you work hard on yourself and develop the manners and integrity, you will become more valuable to the marketplace—and in every area of your life. Your whole life can explode into change. Promotions, no problem. Money, no problem. Economics, no problem. Future, no problem.

You don't need to change things "out there." Don't try to change the seed, don't change the soil, don't change the sunshine, don't change the rain, don't change the mix of seasons. Let the miracle of everything that's available work for you and start working inside you. Work on your philosophy. Work on your attitude. Work on your personality. Work on your language. Work on the gift of communication. Work on all of your abilities. And if you'll start making those personal changes, everything else will change for you—for your benefit and profit.

All values must be defended. Social values, political values, friendship values, marriage values, family values, business values. If you don't develop this skill, you'll never wind up with anything of value. Take full responsibility for what happens to you—which is one of the highest forms of human maturity, the best of human maturity. I'm not saying it's easy; I'm saying it's the best.

There are four major lessons in life to learn and I go into more detail about these in my book *How to Have Your Best Year Ever*. But here I want to give you the gist, as each is vital when navigating your future:

1. *Handle the winters of life*. There are economic winters, social winters, personal winters. Winters when your heart is smashed into a thousand pieces. Wintertime disappointments are common. You must learn how to handle difficulty, which always comes after opportunity. Don't get bogged down; rather, choose to get stronger, wiser, and better. Remember, "Don't wish it was easier, wish you were better. Don't wish for fewer problems, wish for more skills. Don't wish for less challenge, wish for more wisdom."

2. *Take advantage of the spring*. Spring is called opportunity. Opportunity follows difficulty. Expansion follows recession. And all with regularity, you can count on it. But just because spring comes after winter, there's no sign you're going to look good in the fall unless you do something with the opportunities that arise. Only a handful of springs are handed to you. Whatever you want to do with your life, get at it. Don't let the season pass you by.

3. *Nourish and protect yourself and your future in summertime*. Develop your strengths to prevent the intruder from taking the good you've built. Here on this planet, good will be attacked and you must be prepared to defend what is yours. Let reality be your best beginning; not to think so is naïve.

4. *Reap the harvest without complaint*. You are responsible for a healthy personal development season—as well as a season that may lack the expected fruit. We must take personal responsibility

for the harvest—be it good or not so good. No excuses. One of the best indications of human maturity is when you realize that no apology is expected if you've done well, and no complaint if you haven't done well.

MURPHY'S LAW

One of Murphy's Laws says that "If anything can go wrong, it will go wrong." I can attest that anything can happen. I've fallen out of the sky so many times. One time I lost all I had. It was devastating and took me a while to get over that one. Everyone has disappointments. Disappointments are not special gifts reserved for the poor. The question is, what are you going to do about it? Complain? Blame something or someone else? Ignore it? Exaggerate it? No. You're going to take responsibility for it and then figure out a solution, a way around it to move forward.

You're going to skillfully and carefully attack the same problem that has kept you from doing very well, or kept you beneath your potential, or kept you off balance as to your own self-worth. It is so easy to mistake appearances for reality, to confuse the symptom with the real cause.

So what can you do with economic chaos? What can you do with massive disappointment when it's all gone wrong? What can you do when it won't work, when you've run out of money, when you don't feel well, and it's all gone sour? What can you do? Well, let me give you the broad answer first. People can do the most amazing things with the most impossible and disastrous circumstances.

Humans are remarkable—different from all other creations. Human beings can turn weeds into gardens. Humans can turn nothing into something, pennies into fortune, disaster into success. And the reason they can do such remarkable things is because they actually are remarkable. You can reach down inside of you and come up with the answer, the solution, the explanation, the way out. With the gifts you already have, you can change anything you wish to change. And I challenge you to do that.

The process of change is not just a philosophical pronouncement. It takes more than that and it takes more than enthusiasm. It takes a new excitement and personal development and discipline.

Get excited about your ability to make yourself do what's necessary to get a desired result. That's true excitement—not just optimistic panic. True excitement.

NEW HABITS

What could you do starting today that would make a great big positive difference in your life? Answer, a lot! What will most people start doing today? Nothing new. And that's disappointing. What we can do is not in question. What we can do is fantastic and unbelievable! But we settle for disappointing. What we become leads to all the good things. And the habits we form—habits of mind, attitude, and behavior—are a dominant part of what we are becoming.

I understand as well as anyone that forming new habits doesn't come easy, but new habits will come when we change. It is usually not in one cataclysmic explosion, but rather by changing small pieces and parts at a time. I think that's how most of us change. We just keep nudging ourselves in the right direction, forming one or two new habits at a time little by little until finally we've made the turn. And this is where the good life comes from—personal changes and habits.

Wishing we could change is a beginning. Then the wish must be translated into activity, and inspiration and affirmation must lead to discipline. We can affirm that we are going to change, but we must now form new habits and develop new disciplines for the affirmation to come true. Make sure your activities are not going in the opposite direction of your affirmation.

Personal development includes your physical, mental, and spiritual self.

Personal development includes your physical, spiritual, and mental self. Regarding the physical part of you, take good care of yourself. The Bible says we should treat our bodies as if a temple. It's the only place you have to live in—so keep yourself healthy by exercising, eating good food, and resting. It's a temple, not a woodshed.

The spiritual side of our development includes your values and your virtues. If you believe in spirituality, my advice is to study it and practice it. Don't let it go unnourished if you do believe. That's my best advice on the spiritual side.

Another part of the personal development challenge is to expand yourself mentally. Learn, study, grow, change, educate yourself, become more knowledgeable. Take time to feed your mind, nourish your mind. Some people read so little that they couldn't give you a good strong argument as to their own personal beliefs.

You have to know what you believe, what your philosophy of life is. And you have to be able to defend it. If you can't defend your virtues and if you can't defend your values, you'll fall prey to philosophies that are not in your best interests.

CASE IN POINT

I was a millionaire by age 31. I was broke by age 33—two and a half million dollars all swept away by making foolish decisions. That first money was really hard to keep as a young guy. I fell for some of the temptations. As the saying goes, "A fool and his money are soon parted." I was recklessness and made some unwise business decisions. A condensed version of the story is that a company wanted to borrow some money, quarter of a million, and wanted me to personally sign as a guarantor. I knew the company could pay it back, so I signed. I'm the hero.

A little later the company got in financial trouble, went back, and borrowed a quarter of a million again. I signed the first note, it was all paid back, and I decided not to sign the second time. However, within a year this company went belly up and I got a letter from the bank wanting a quarter of a million because I was still on the loan as the guarantor! Even though I never signed the second note, the originally signed note was a "continuing guarantee."

Through that and a few other experiences, some of my newfound wealth that was on paper disappeared. From poor to rich and from rich back to poor—what now? It occurred to me that even though my money was gone, I still had the skills. And the skills proved to be more valuable than the money. So I just simply went back to work, went back using the formula I had used in the first place to do well—and I made many times more than what I did the first time. That's the key! You must go back to work.

I was willing to readjust my lifestyle. The fancy cars and homes had to go—all that stuff had to go. I went back to a modest apartment and started over rather than putting up a façade as if nothing had changed. Circumstances did indeed change and all I could do was change myself, my choices, and my outlook.

From that experience and keeping the right attitude, I was stronger than I was the first time around or the second time around. This can be true for you as well if faced with financial loss. Everything comes down to attitude and philosophy. If you have the right attitude, no matter what happens, if you just readjust your attitude and philosophy and adopt a whole new mindset—you can absolutely start again and be successful again.

Some of the great fortunes are made after a person turns 50 or 60. And the reason is because with all the ups and downs in those accumulation of years, now when an idea or a new burst of vitality or goals set in, these people have a load of experience to invest. That's why these fortunes become incredible even in later years.

When you're 20, you don't have much experience to invest, but you can still do okay and climb the ladder fairly quickly. And when you're 30, you have a bit more experience to invest if something happened and you had to start over. But in your 50s or 60s, you have a good handful of years of experience to invest, which may make all the difference in the world.

It's true you can tip either way—to be discouraged by it all or to be inspired by it all. And that's part of the mystery. After a loss, you can turn around and make another fortune. The mystery also is not everybody will turn around and make another fortune. Some will use the loss as a reason to succeed. Others use it as a reason to give up. Same circumstances.

I mention this story frequently because it's true and it's an excellent example. Researchers followed two boys, twins. The father of these boys was a scoundrel and a drunk. As they followed the two boys, later in life one turned out to be a scoundrel and a drunk. And they asked him, "Why did your life turn out like this?" And he said, "Well, what would you expect? My father was a scoundrel and a drunk." The other boy turned out to be a professional doing very well. And they asked him, "How did you turn out to be a professional?" And he said, "I didn't want to be like my father." Same father, two different choices.

One used his father as an excuse for living a poorer life, and the other one used it as a reason to live a full, rich life. A large portion of our life is shaped by attitude and influence, including the people near us.

Good questions to ask yourself are: *Who are the people closest to me? What kind of influence do they have on me? Positive or negative?*

Your associations can make all the difference in the world in your future. We have to practice limited associations. Some people you can be around a few hours but not a few days. And some people you can be around a few minutes but not a few hours. And then some people, you have to walk away from. And sometimes, it's helpful if somebody comes along and helps us in a moment of stress or distress and offers a book or advice, or they just say, "I'll be here if you need me."

Make some good friends so that no matter what happens, when things turn upside down, you'll have people to rely on for wise counsel. I've had some of those in my life. They've helped save my life, save my career, save everything. Walk the beach or the dusty paths with someone who cares about you and is an excellent friend, someone you can be honest with so together you can try and sort it all out. Whether personal, family, or business troubles, there's no way to put a value on that type of friendship—it's so very valuable.

Learning new strategies and making new habits is like the sailboat. The wind blows on every sailboat, but the difference in destination is the set of the sail, not the blowing of the wind. Some winds are contrary, some are severe, some are easy, some are gentle. So the same wind blows on us all. The difference in where we arrive three years from now is not the blowing of the wind, it's the set of the sail. Philosophy, attitude, willingness to do the basics and fundamentals to make a new start.

Go again.

ABSOLUTE TRUST

Many, many years ago, I had a unique experience that developed for me something called *absolute trust*. I can't really explain it. It's probably more of a mystery to me than it is a reality. But it's there. And it helped to establish my very simple theology. And my simple theology goes like this: number one, I believe God is just, which means I'm probably in trouble; number two, I believe God's mercy endures forever, which means I probably have an excellent chance. Having absolute trust in Someone is an incredible feeling. Better even than being financially independent.

My father said, "Son, someday you have to know this incredible feeling that nobody and nothing has a claim on you or your assets." He said, "It's an incredible feeling. And until you get there, you really don't know what it's like. No one can tell you." And I think that's true of absolute trust—it is so unique. I don't even know how to teach it. All I know is it wonderfully happened for me all those years ago. And it helps me, even with my high profile and busy chase around the world to share ideas, life. Absolute trust gives me an underlying serenity that is absolutely incredible. It makes the days busy, but peaceful. It makes the months highly active, but keeps me anchored. It's astonishing.

I think the seeds of the idea and the experience came from my parents who laid this superb foundation for me when I was growing up. So, I've lived an extraordinary life. And if I was to pick one thing that I think serves me so well in traveling the world, talking to people, being an entrepreneur, busy as can be, hopefully for another 40 years, it is this belief in absolute trust.

I believe that this little phrase is helpful for everyone—if you can finally come to the conclusion that *God's in control*. Once I really believed that, I started sleeping like a baby.

Knowing God is in control makes worry obsolete. On the other hand, if you're in the midst of a battle and you walk into the general's tent and he's sobbing, it's time to worry. Knowing that ultimately you have absolute trust in God, that God's in control, makes life all the more enjoyable, in every circumstance.

I know that however He has designed for it all to work out is fine with me. And if it seems turbulent and if it doesn't seem to fit together at the moment, I can get through that easily with the faith I have in God. Faith is when you don't have any facts or anything to prove. If everything could be proven by facts and figures, you wouldn't need faith. Faith is an extraordinary human possibility to see things that don't exist, to believe when there don't seem to be any facts to support—that's when trust, absolute trust and faith impacts your life.

5

ATTITUDE AND AMBITION AND...

ATTITUDE

First of all, we're affected by what we know. Second, we're affected by how we feel about what we know—the emotional part. There are many different ways to feel reflected in our attitude—our response to situations. For example, someone says, "If this is all I'm getting paid, I'm not coming early and I'm not staying late on the job." That is his choice of attitude. If that guy has that same attitude for the next five years, would it greatly affect his future paydays? The answer is, of course. No one can escape the accumulated effect their attitude. No one.

How do we engage in the kind of philosophical thinking that refines our attitude to give us a chance for future fortune rather than what will be missing in the future? We can change our attitude with making a conscious effort to change our minds, our outlook. For example, the same guy could adopt this attitude: "No matter what they pay, I always come early and I always stay late, to invest in my own future." Why would one person have a pessimistic attitude and another person have an optimistic attitude? We call that mysteries of the mind, right? I don't know.

Everyone chooses for themselves what their attitude is about this or that. For instance, if you don't know what the consequences are going to be, it could be very easy to choose the wrong attitude and not discipline yourself to the right attitude.

So a big portion of our life is affected by how we feel. The following is a brief list about the feelings that affect our lives.

1. HOW YOU FEEL ABOUT THE PAST.

It's easy to carry the past as a burden instead of as a school. It's easy to let the past overwhelm you instead of let the past instruct you. How to feel about past hurts and losses and difficulties and the times you failed and the times that didn't work—the accumulation of all those feelings will greatly affect your future.

2. HOW YOU FEEL ABOUT THE FUTURE.

Our life is affected by price and promise. And it's not easy to pay the price if you can't see the promise. I think kids are having problems these days trying to pay the price because they can't see the promise, but all of us wouldn't mind paying the price if we could have a clear view of tomorrow, next week, next month, next year. If we had the high assurance with great probability of how it was going to work out, do you think we would hesitate to pay? The answer is no, but everybody hesitates to pay if the future isn't clear. My karate instructor said, "Mr. Rohn, you can't believe the incredible feeling of walking down any city street unafraid." I said, "Let's get on with the classes." I will sweat and put myself through the paces with that extraordinary promise in front of me. Would you crack open the books? Burn the midnight oil? Engage in the extra thoughts and disciplines if the promise was adequate? Of course.

3. HOW YOU FEEL ABOUT EACH OTHER.

Your attitude about society, country, state and city, community, family, enterprise, office, company, corporation, and division is very important. To have a unique understanding about other human beings and what makes a good life is what constitutes a good life. *You can't succeed by yourself.* So to have a unique refined sense of appreciation for each other is prerequisite. It takes each other to build a society. It takes all of us to build a country, to build a nation. It takes all of us to build a community. I gave a speech and I was unusually affected by the Pledge of Allegiance that day. Big strong voices. It was going through my mind the next few days, and I thought, *What an important key document, the Pledge of Allegiance.* So I started writing a discourse on the Pledge of Allegiance. For each keyword I wrote a little summary for our Tape of the Month Club. The Pledge of Allegiance is unique— starting with "I," and ending with "All."

It takes all of us to make any one of us successful, and a uniquely refined appreciation of the *all of us* is what makes the *I of us* do much better. That appreciation of society takes all of us to make a market. We need each other's ideas and inspiration. When you have the sense of appreciation of the *all* of us, now you and your place, your possibilities, and your opportunities start to really soar when you understand how important it is within the framework of the all of us. You can't succeed by yourself; it's hard to find a rich hermit.

4. HOW YOU FEEL ABOUT YOURSELF.

Understanding self-worth is the beginning of progress. How valuable are you? What could you do if you had all the skills? What true value could you become? This is one of the better exercises. Ask yourself: *What could I become in terms of value? What could I really do in the marketplace, in enterprise, family, home, love, experience, marriage, friendship? How valuable could I become? Am I valuable enough to work on what all is still not functioning in my life to full capacity? If I'm operating at 20 percent, what could I possibly do with the other 80 percent? Do I have it in knowledge and worth and value and experience?* Once you start understanding this part of you, understanding how valuable you are, it is a whole new experience, understanding self-worth. Attitude plays a big, major part in how your life works out.

AMBITION

You are more than your ambition. These are undoubtedly some of the most valuable words in this program on the power of ambition. You can't serve your ambition. No, your ambition must serve you. If you serve your ambition, you become less than your ambition. If you don't allow your ambition to serve you, your ambition won't have any resources to pull from, to grow, to maintain. It won't have a reservoir of strength and discipline and ingenuity and creativity. If you serve your ambition, it will be weakened. There will be nothing to revive it, replenish it.

So how do you ensure that your ambition is serving you? Let's look at the methods and principles for building your ambition, the building blocks, the fundamental philosophies that we must continue to work on so our healthy and beneficial ambition will continue to serve us and work for us. These following building blocks will help you develop the foundation of good, strong ambition:

1. POSITIVE SELF-DIRECTION

Positive self-direction says, "I know who I am. I know where I want to go. I'm working on my plan to get there." In positive self-direction, you accumulate knowledge and experiences and feelings and philosophies. You need to gather all that you can to help you decide where you want to go, how you want to get there, and how to keep on track.

2. SELF-RELIANCE

Self-reliance is taking responsibility for your own life; taking full responsibility for whatever happens to you; taking the credit and or the blame for the result of yesterday's activities; changing what's in your power to change; being responsible; working with others by doing all you can to bring the most value to the table and the marketplace; being self-reliant and responsible.

3. SELF-ENTERPRISE

Keep your eyes open and your mind active to recognize an opportunity and to grasp it; consistently create opportunity;

be disciplined enough and prepared enough to take advantage of the opportunities around you. An enterprising attitude says, "Find out before action is taken. Do your homework, do the research, be prepared, be resourceful, do all you can in preparation for what will inevitably come to you, what you're preparing to come to you."

4. WORKING WITH OTHERS

Building your ambition is manifested by working with others, being able to share the spotlight, keeping your ego in your back pocket, and giving others credit when credit is due. Caring enough about others to offer a kind word, a thoughtful gesture, a helping hand. A country can't be built by one person. A company can't be built with one person. A family can't be built with one person. A friendship can't be built with one person. Each of us needs all of us to succeed. Learn to work with others to achieve your goals, to finish your tasks.

5. SELF-APPRECIATION

You must develop a strong appreciation for the conclusions you have made, for the sail you have set, for the philosophies you have adopted, for your own methods, your own style, your own model of success. Remember that success is the steady progress toward your own personal goals, and self-appreciation is crucial in keeping you moving toward those goals.

Those are the five principles necessary to build your ambition—plus one, *courage*.

COURAGE

As you take your metaphorical chisel in hand to discover and create the various qualities of character within yourself, you may need this one perhaps more than all the others—*courage*.

Since ancient times, philosophers have seen courage as the basis of all real achievement. There's a book that tells the stories of all the winners of the United States Congressional Medal of Honor. It's a book that will bring tears to your eyes. It's one of the most powerful documents ever written.[3] One American after another who put aside all thought of safety and faced down death in the service of this country. And more often than not, it's been in order to save other Americans rather than to defeat an enemy. When you read of their exploits, you realize that these were people who simply lost their fear of death to do what had to be done.

Yes, those Medal of Honor winners were courageous individuals, but by itself, is overcoming the fear of death necessarily an expression of courage? I don't doubt that there are many people in this country who break the law and aren't afraid to die in the process, but I wouldn't call them courageous. And there are people who deliberately do foolhardy things with their cars that jeopardize their own lives and the lives of others, but they aren't courageous people. We might not be able to precisely define it, but we intuitively sense that there are some differences between acts of rashness and the accomplishments of those winners of the Congressional Medal of Honor.

Let me sum up in a couple of sentences what those differences reveal about the true nature of courage. I can't put it any better than the Greek philosopher Aristotle did more than 2,000 years ago: "A truly courageous person is not some-one who never feels fear, but who fears the right thing at the right time in the right way." What exactly does that mean? What does it mean to fear the right thing in the right way at the right time? To find the answer, let's look at some specific sources of fear that many individuals are facing right now.

FEAR

First, a great many people today are afraid of what might happen to them financially, and it's certainly true that great changes are taking place in the economy that will have a direct impact on the lives of millions of people. I've heard it said that a corporation that employs 10,000 men and women today may only need one-fifth that many within 10 years. Over the past 50 years, whole sections of our society have learned to identify with the corporation that employed them. That corporation provided not only a salary but health bene-fits and the opportunity to create a pension fund that would make retirement possible at age 65 or even sooner.

Now that relationship between the employer and the cor-poration is changing. Much of the work that used to be done by domestic workers can now be done more cheaply overseas or with immigrants, and companies are taking advantage of that, perhaps out of necessity, perhaps simply to fatten the bottom line. In any case, people's fear of losing their job has now reached many segments of the workforce.

What else are we afraid of? Many people are concerned about their health. They're afraid of getting sick because they don't exercise enough or they're eating the wrong foods or the chemicals in the air or in their food or water. In fact, I think people today are even more frightened than they were in the past when disease and poor sanitation were everywhere. And with regard to their health, people are also afraid of the expenses that might result if they or a family member would become sick or disabled.

So financial fears and health-related fears are two of our major concerns—but something else I sense really scares people today is a bit less easy to categorize. It's a general feeling that things aren't as good as they used to be, that there's a loss of control at some basic level of our society. There's a sense that one earthquake after another, some large and obvious, some smaller and almost imperceptible, have accumulated to shift the foundations of society and it's going to keep shifting toward a result that's anything but good.

Now keeping in mind our idea that a courageous person is not someone who never feels fear, but who fears the right thing at the right time in the right way, let's ask ourselves if these fears really fit that definition. If we look a little deeper, we see that what really scares people is the sense that they're going to be helpless, that they placed their trust in somebody or something and were let down and can't do anything about it. They feel helpless.

But remember, you're never really helpless and you should refuse to accept that mindset. You are never a victim of circumstances. No matter what happens, you're never without options that can get you back on track. It takes courage to recognize that, because it means accepting responsibility for your own future, but I suggest we accept that responsibility because no one is going to accept it for us—no matter what we may have been led to believe.

Every generation has faced insecurities **and lived with them and triumphed over them.**

Let me emphasize that underlying most fears is the fear of helplessness—of being victimized or being blown around by the winds of fate like a leaf is blown off a tree—but is that really a legitimate way of looking at life? To me, it sounds like being afraid of the dark; in which case, the best thing to do is to get yourself up out of bed and switch on the light.

After all, the people who built this country didn't feel helpless when they faced obstacles that we can't even imagine today. I'm not saying we should all just gather around the campfire and tell stories about George Washington, but we should realize that every generation has faced insecurities and lived with them and triumphed over them.

Only in the past 50 years or so, people have come to expect a life without any tough times and real difficulties. But adversity isn't something to fear; it's something to expect, something to prepare for, and something to overcome.

The truly courageous person is not immune to fear, but it plays a different role in his or her life than it does for other people. If you're a courageous person, your fears aren't about what someone might do to you or something that might happen to you. Your fears are about not living up to your ideals, about reacting instead of acting, about not taking advantage of the opportunities that are always within reach.

A truly courageous person is not afraid of what might or might not happen next week or next year. A courageous person fears not making the most of every moment today. Truly courageous people fear the impulse to dominate other people. They lead by helping others to be their best. Truly courageous people fear making appearances more important than realities, making impressions more important than communication, making themselves more important than those who are depending on them.

But there's one thing a courageous person fears most. Have you ever seen a deer caught in the headlights of a car? How the deer just stands there as though paralyzed with fear, not knowing what to do or which way to go? The truly courageous person fears getting caught like that. So a constant part of his or her life is dedicated to making sure it never happens.

When it comes to wanting things, there's never any such thing as enough, and that can really get on our nerves. You get a new car, but in a couple of years, it's an old car. You get a new computer, it does everything real fast, certainly faster than the one your neighbor has, but then a year goes by and now your neighbor gets a computer that's even faster than yours. Where does it all end?

WISDOM

There's really only one kind of person who's actually comfortable with the impossibility of satisfying his or her appetites. This is the person who wants that mysterious commodity called *wisdom,* whatever that is, and wants it more than all the cars and computers in the world. Wisdom, like the learning capacity of the human brain, is infinite. There will always be more to know and there will always be plenty of room in your brain for everything you learn.

Life is a paradise, really, if you're a person who genuinely wants wisdom.

We all want to be successful and I'm certainly in favor of that, but I've known some people who literally wanted all the money they could get, not what the money could buy, but the money itself, the greenbacks, quarters, dimes, nickels. Even if he had rooms filled with thousand-dollar bills, he'd still want the next person's nickel and he'd be in pain about that, filled with envy about it.

On the other hand, the person who wants wisdom also looks back over his shoulder, but he just wants to see what the other guy is reading; and if the other guy is reading a book he hasn't read yet, he looks forward to reading it himself.

The acquisition of wisdom is not what all the mathematicians call a zero-sum game. When one person shares wisdom with another, neither person is diminished. In fact, both are made wiser. Giving and taking is such a basic experience for most of us, but the whole concept of giving and taking doesn't really apply to wisdom. There's no giving and taking—there's only sharing.

True sources of wisdom lie within ourselves.

There are plenty of people who are too smart for their own good, people who are filled to overflowing with facts and technical knowledge, but who are sadly lacking in human understanding and common sense. We've all met people like that. They score high on all the tests, they get perfect grades in school, they win all the prizes. They often get paid very well to practice their skills to build things and write computer programs and carry on lawsuits and manage other people's affairs.

But go home with one of these whizzes. Look at their lives outside of work, if they have a life outside their work, and you'll most probably find that they lack in basic common sense. Most of them don't really give any thought to the difference between right and wrong and what's fair and how to enjoy happiness and what life is worth.

"What's that got to do with me?" the smart one asks. "What is this thing you call common sense and human wisdom and a strong character?" I've seen people who have everything they could possibly want, every object you could dream of, everything you can drive down the street or sail on the ocean or fly through the air—but inside where the real person lives, they're broke. They have nothing. They haven't got a clue of what is really valuable in life.

TWO WISE MEN

The Bible tells us that King Solomon was the wisest man in the whole world, but he was not only the wisest, he was also the richest man in the world. Kings and queens came from around the world seeking Solomon's advice and to admire his riches. Solomon was just a young man living in the court of King David, his father, and God told him He would grant him one wish. Solomon didn't wish for a kingdom or great power or good looks or unlimited pleasure or long life or love or fame or security. Solomon asked God to grant him wisdom; and because he asked only for wisdom, God gave him everything else too.

The most important difference between you and me and Solomon isn't where or when we were born or the privileges we have or don't. The difference isn't in our names or our bank accounts or the positions we hold in life. The difference is Solomon got wisdom by asking God for it. The rest of us must look around for wisdom and look for it in everything we read and in everything we do and in everyone we meet. And most of all—we must look for wisdom in ourselves.

The wisest man in ancient Greece and actually the world was Socrates. People would ask Socrates, "What is wisdom?" He always gave the same answer, "I don't know." In fact, Socrates never claimed to know much of anything, except how to ask questions. And by asking questions, he proved that the people didn't know what they thought they knew or were certain of.

Everybody in Greece agreed that Socrates was the wisest man in Greece, but unlike King Solomon, the philosopher Socrates didn't have great wealth. The wisest man in Greece was poor. King Solomon managed a huge household with many wives and homes and lots of children, and he accomplished this without any discord or unhappiness, but Socrates had no home life at all.

The wisest man in Greece was married to a famous and terrible nag, and they had no children. Socrates went to the marketplace every day and hung around and asked people questions and hoped to get invited to a banquet so he wouldn't have to go home and face his wife.

King Solomon was honored by all the great leaders of his time, but Socrates didn't even have any support among the powerful people in his own country. Their sons would go to Socrates and learn what they could from the philosopher, but the powerful families of Athens, where Socrates lived, got tired of Socrates's questions. They grew exasperated with the way he taught the youth of Greece—that nobody knows anything for sure. So they accused the wisest man in Greece of corrupting their children.

Instead of honoring the greatest philosopher who ever lived, the Athenians sentenced Socrates to death unless he would take back what he taught, unless he would apologize. But Socrates didn't take it back. He didn't apologize. Rather, Socrates drank down a cup of poison and just sat there calmly saying goodbye to his few faithful students, asking questions the whole time.

Solomon and Socrates—two very wise men with two very different destinies. Great wisdom is no guarantee of anything, but to those who really care about it, wisdom is its own reward.

Part of wisdom is knowing what you lack and looking for it and asking for it. Another part of wisdom is knowing at the same time as you ask that there are no final answers, there are always more questions, there are always more things and people you don't now know and haven't yet heard of or seen.

So you may have that retirement package, you may have the medical benefits, the pension, the sunbelt home, and a steady income you can live on. What good is it if you're isolated? And I don't mean just physically alone. I mean isolated from a real sense of connection with what's come before and with what lies ahead. It's here that wisdom provides very real, very practical benefits. It's wisdom that provides a sense of life's value and assurance that all the effort has been worthwhile.

A fulfilled life requires meaning as well as substance.

There's no question that we must take care of our material needs, but a fulfilled life requires meaning as well as substance. *Wisdom is the fruit of experience.* Experience is what everyone gets if they live long enough—but not everyone knows what to do with it. Wisdom comes from seeing the world and the people in it and from noticing patterns and connections, and from using what other people let you see of themselves in order to understand your own self.

HUMOR

A duck walked into a store and filled a shopping cart with goods, then pushed the cart up to the checkout area. The clerk took a look at the full shopping cart and said, "Will that be cash or charge?" The duck looked at him a little impatiently and said, "Hey, I'm in kind of a hurry. Just put it all on my bill." Of course that was a joke—an oldie but goodie.

This section is about humor and its role in character and leadership, so I thought it would be a good idea to start off with a joke. In fact, it's almost always a good idea to let people know you have a good sense of humor, because in this society we take humor very seriously. And by the way, you do have a good sense of humor, don't you? I'm confident you'll answer in the affirmative because virtually everyone is sure they have a good sense of humor, and I discuss more about that later.

Right now, I want to emphasize how important humor is as an aspect of strong character while navigating your future. Yet if you were to ask 100 people to name character's most vital elements, I doubt if more than five would refer to humor. In fact, I don't think any would. When he wrote his classic *Study of American Society* in the early 18th century, Alexis de Tocqueville predicted that if the United States ever came to be ruled by a dictator, it would be someone with a well-developed sense of humor. If this is true, it's certainly a very different situation than you would find in any other country in the world. Think of the communist and fascist dictators who played such a major role in 20th century history. They were not exactly a bunch of laugh-a-minute guys. They were good at projecting anger and creating fear, but humor, no.

Americans, however, respond to very different qualities in their leaders, and though they were obviously not dictators or tyrants, it's true that most of our beloved national leaders have had the ability to make others laugh and to laugh at themselves.

Though he was fundamentally a rather melancholy man, Abraham Lincoln was also renowned as a humorist. Every biography of Lincoln refers to his love of funny stories and his willingness to stop and tell a joke even in the midst of important business. And in more recent times, Presidents Franklin Roosevelt, John Kennedy, and Ronald Reagan were able to smooth out the ups and downs of their political careers with humor, and it was often directed at themselves. People could see that these men were strong enough and confident enough to make jokes at their own expense. When we recognize those abilities in a person, we believe they'll also be strong and confident in serious or even dangerous situations.

In short, we as Americans see a well-developed sense of humor as an aspect of a strong character and as almost a prerequisite for leadership. But before you go out and buy a joke book as part of your personal self-development program, here's the bad news. To a great extent, you can't learn to be humorous, and that alone makes humor different from other traits.

Perhaps one reason we respond so strongly to humor in our leaders is because we associate it with honesty, which is well-founded. Real humor is honest because it can't be faked. You can pretend to be serious, just like you can pretend to be intelligent. You can always fake those qualities, and some people do it all the time, but you can't really pretend to be funny.

I suggest that to a large extent, humor is something that you either have or you don't; unlike many other self-development skills, it's very difficult to improve your capacity for humor. But if that's true, doesn't it suggest that there's something self-contradictory about this whole discussion? After all, what's the point of talking so much about humor if there's really very little you can do to toward strengthening your capacity for it?

Well, it may be true that you can't increase the natural proportion of humor in your personality beyond a certain preordained point, but that's not the end of the story. You can still learn to have a basically humorous approach to life, or perhaps playful would be a better word, and I think the ability to do so is an extremely important indicator of strong character.

COMEDY OR TRAGEDY

Life can be either a comedy or a tragedy, and it's always in your power to determine how you want to see it. I prefer to see it as a comedy, and I highly recommend this to you also, but let me explain exactly what I mean by that. I don't mean to suggest that life is a comedy like you see on television at 8 o'clock on Channel 5. I'm using comedy according to the classical definition of the term—as a progression from sadness to happiness, from a low point to a high point, from poverty to wealth in every sense.

We live in a time that equates seriousness with intelligence, unhappiness with sensitivity, and victimization with moral authority. In short, we have largely chosen to see life as tragic rather than comic, but to the extent you participate in this mindset, I believe you are limiting your potential for success in the material sense; and even more importantly, you are doing nothing for your character, or at least nothing good.

Humor can be your best tool for distancing yourself from the negativity and pessimism that's so rampant today. It's not always an easy tool to use, but I believe its importance has been seriously underestimated as an element of strong character.

HONESTY AND INTEGRITY

Honesty and integrity are two qualities of a strong character that are fairly easy to define: Say what you mean, mean what you say. Do what you say you are going to do when you say you're going to do it. That's integrity. A clear correspondence between words and deeds. Don't lie, tell the truth. That's honesty. Despite the fact that these are some of the clearest, most easily recognized elements of strong character, in the real world they're also some of the most difficult to find. It seems it's always been that way.

The ancient Greek philosopher Demosthenes went searching for an honest man and he never found one. I've been fortunate. I've known a great many honest people, but if I measured that number up against all the less-than-ethical people I've encountered, I'd have to admit that even in my experience, honesty and integrity are rather rare. Why is that? I hope to provide some answers, but just as our discussion of courage began with a look at fear, I want to start talking about honesty by looking at the exact opposite of honest behavior.

There was a time when telling a lie was very serious business. Those were the days before lawsuits and legally enforceable contracts. It was also very serious to accuse someone of lying. Today, a breach of integrity in a business matter might mean calling in the lawyers; but for hundreds of years in the past, calling someone a liar was the most common way to provoke a dual, at first with swords, later with pistols.

Dishonesty was treated like a personal insult that demanded immediate redress. Everyone knew the big problems that could result if you got caught, so lying to another person took a certain amount of foolish bravery. But there's no such risk today, is there? Some people lie all the time without thinking about it. Most people know when they're being lied to, which they may find irritating, but they just accept it. Maybe they decide to become liars themselves. In any case, very few duels are being fought.

To explain this, we can compare between how some people today feel about lying and how they feel about money. It used to be you either had money or you didn't. When you bought something and the bill came, you had to pay it or there was an immediate problem. There were only two alternatives. You took care of your debts or you were a thief. Some people would take their own lives if they couldn't honor their debts. I'm sure we agree that's not exactly true any longer.

Many people don't feel the same kind of personal responsibility about paying debts promptly. And today, of course, we can put off paying for our purchases as long as we can make the minimum payment on our credit card. Of course, there's a high rate of interest on that debt and the balance due can quickly mount up, but most people don't even think about that. It's a price they're willing to pay to have exactly what they want right now.

There are many situations where it's painful to tell the truth. It's painful in just the same way that paying a big fat bill is painful. In fact, we even use the same words to talk about paying debts and telling the truth. We may talk about somebody's word being like "money in the bank." We talk about being held accountable, about having to account for yourself, about being called to account.

If you've done something that you're not proud of and you're called to account for it, well, what does that feel like? How do you handle it? What are your options when you have to explain something that makes you uncomfortable? Well, it's a bit like that moment of decision when the credit card bill comes every month. If you want to pay off the whole balance, there may be some pain and sacrifice involved. You know your life will be simpler in the long run, but it's going to hurt a little right now to pay off the new golf clubs or the new computer.

Gritting your teeth and paying in full can hurt, so quite often it seems easier to pay the minimum and delay the pain until next month. It's easier to float your financial truth off into a little imaginary plastic flying carpet and sail it into the mailbox. Of course, it's more like a boomerang that will come back around and hit you in the back of the head someday. But as

Scarlett O'Hara said, "I'll think about that tomorrow." For the time being, it's gone with the wind.

Let me give you some good advice about avoiding a bankrupt character. Pay your ethical debts. Keep your integrity intact, face ugly realities with the truth as soon as they appear. When you feel that temptation to hedge, resist it immediately. Don't treat it casually. Treat it like a grease fire in the kitchen that you have to put out before it burns down your house or fills the whole place with so much smoke that you can't see where you're going anymore. That's exactly what will happen when your ethical capital runs out. You won't see where you're going.

Maybe you think I'm being a bit tough here. Am I really saying that in every instance, you have to tell the truth, the whole truth, and nothing but the truth? No, that's not what I mean. In fact, I think there are many times when you need some flexibility with the whole truth, which we will discuss later. Outright lying, however, planned lying, lying with an ulterior motive, lying for personal gain—that kind of lying is definitely wrong.

Untruthfulness is so tempting today. I want to make a clear distinction between what I call foolish, stupid, or silly lying and lying that is downright evil and poisonous to the character. Boasting, bombast, blarney, bragging—these are all the same. They're always floating around in the atmosphere and can affect you at any time, like catching a cold. They're mostly harmless unless you start building a whole personality around them, which has definitely happened to some people.

Someone else scored a game-winning touchdown back in high school; but while you're watching the Super Bowl with your neighbor, you say that you caught the pass. Now consider this scenario. You really don't know Joe, the president of XYZ corporation. You were introduced to him one time, but the client you're trying to impress has never even shaken hands with Joe, so here's a chance to score some points. This is all just hot air, boasting—and it's all going on your credit card. All of this is childish trash talk, and it's usually spontaneous. It comes from succumbing to a moment of social pressure. It's not the kind of behavior that defines strong character.

If a supervisor in a corporation steals one of his subordinate's ideas and takes credit for it in the eyes of the CEO, that requires a whole chain of events and a conscious decision to keep the deception going through the various links in the chain. That kind of lying is theft. It's not only theft of the subordinate's idea, it's stealing from the CEO too. It's stealing the CEO's sense of reality. It's creating an illusion. If someone falsifies an earnings report to inflate the price of a company's stock, that's deliberately creating a mirage in the minds of the investors. In the real world, both these examples have happened, and many times lives and careers have been ruined.

It's been my experience that those who engage in serious lying and unethical behavior get caught one way or the other. Usually the people who are being deceived awaken from the illusions; but even if this never happens, the criminal, and I don't think that's too strong a word, has to buy into the illusion so deeply himself that his own sense of reality is eroded. By trying to loosen other people's grasp of the truth, you end up losing your own.

All of it, small-time lying and big time deceit, comes from fear. Somebody is afraid the truth about themselves isn't good enough, so they depart from the truth. Trust who you really are. Trust your ability to earn the respect of others. Pay whatever price the truth costs. Pay that bill immediately—because in the long run, it's a real bargain.

As Shakespeare wrote, "All the world's a stage," and to some extent we're all playing roles, but being honest and having integrity can make life so much more enjoyable. This is where ethics and psychology really overlap. Not only is it right to minimize cognitive dissonance. In the long run, it's a lot easier on your psyche.

You may know someone who got ahead as a result of dishonest or unethical behavior. When you're a kid, you think that never happens, but when you get older, you realize it does. Then you see the long-term consequences of dishonest gain and see that it doesn't pay in the end. I've seen people who made millions with questionable business tactics, and I've also seen a higher percentage of health problems among those people than any insurance actuary could possibly account for.

"Hope of dishonest gain is the beginning of loss." I don't think that old saying refers to the loss of money; I think it means loss of self-respect. You can have all the material things in the world, but if you've lost respect for yourself, what do you really have? The only way to attain success and enjoy it is to achieve it honestly, and with pride in what you've done. Hey, that's not just a sermon, that's very practical advice that you can take to heart *and* to the bank.

NOTE

1. *United States of America Congressional Medal of Honor Recipients and Their Official Citations* (Minneapolis, MN: Highland House II, Inc., 2002).

6

INGREDIENTS FOR DRAMATIC LIFE CHANGE

I've learned over the years that some, if not most, of the ingredients for dramatic life changes include other people. I urge you to take the following advice to heart and you will see substantial and positive changes in your life while helping others. *Help people* with:

- Their lives, not just their jobs or the job skills.
- Sharing a book, a poem, advice.
- Words of praise, encouragement, something meaningful.
- Setting their goals and expressing their dreams.
- Seeing a successful future.
- Guidance if errors or mistakes have been made.
- Listening when having relationship issues.
- Improving their communication skills.
- Building good, solid, profitable lives.

PROFITS ARE BETTER THAN WAGES

An ingredient that changed my life forever was this phrase: *profits are better than wages*. Once I understood that truth, I got rich, very wealthy. Profits are better than wages—no one taught me that in high school. I went to college for a year and a half and I never heard it there either. I came to realize that wages make you a living, which is fine. Profits make you a fortune, which is super fine. It's up to you to live fine or super fine.

I taught capitalism when I was in Moscow and was amazed at how wrong the communists' philosophy was. They thought capitalism meant big companies that oppress its workers, which was and is absolutely ridiculous. Communism taught that capital (assets of every kind) belongs to the state, not the people. And, of course, we taught and teach that capital (assets of every kind) belongs in the hands of the people, not the state.

In the United States, it doesn't take much to start an enterprise that makes a profit. I teach kids to have two bicycles—one to ride and one to rent. With a little ingenuity, you're on your way to profits. So profits are better than wages. Capitalism is better than communism.

Communism says people are too dumb and stupid to know what to do with capital, so the government must take capital away from the people and give it to the all-wise, all-knowing government to manage and allocate. Communism has devastated every country it dominates. It took East Germany more than a trillion dollars to clean up after communism was overturned and reunified with West Germany in 1990. Capital belongs in the hands of the people because that is where the ingenuity is—that is where people can bring ideas and goods and services to the marketplace for the benefit of all people. Once I understood this fact of human and economic nature, it was so incredible—profits are better than wages.

To complete your life-changing recipe, there are a few other critical ingredients that can make the difference.

The ingredient of *curiosity* is wanting to know—and of course that starts early as children, but it's important to be curious throughout your life, to be curious about what's happening. Be curious about human beings and human behavior, curious about yourself. Be curious about government, politics, society, banking, money, the military, taxes, what makes things work? What makes a city work? What makes a government work?

I remember years ago someone mentioned Russia might conquer China. I said, "If you conquer China, what the heck would you do with it?" Curiosity is trying to comprehend how the world works, how industry and trade works. I remember going to Manhattan for the first time. I was so awestruck being in this huge city. One thing that came to my mind was, *How does this city work? How does everything and everyone blend together? How does everybody get fed and all the commerce take place? How can the lettuce in my salad be so fresh here in the middle of a city? How does all this happen?*

It's a miracle how a city works. It's a miracle how the country works. How does an economy work so that it stays on a steady course? It's amazing. Keep that kind of curiosity active in your mind. Simply be curious about your relationships with other people—when you are sitting at the conference table, be curious about how you could get into the inner circle where they talk about incredible things that affect business, commerce, society, and the world. An important ingredient is your curiosity.

Tony Robbins, who attended my seminars all those years ago, had an incredible attitude, an insatiable appetite for learning. You want to know, to learn, to expand your mind. Reading books is enjoyable. Going to class and taking notes is enjoyable.

Then stir your ingredients into *action*. Don't wait until you've helped everyone, or made all the profits you can, or you know it all, but to do what you know and let the rest unfold and be revealed as you move forward. An illustration: On a foggy night if you can only see 100 feet, then walk that 100 feet and now you can see the next 100 feet. Take it a bit at a time. To start advancing toward your future, take one step at a time.

So now you have as part of your recipe: curiosity, an appetite for learning, and willingness to put it all into activity right away. Then add a willingness to *accept constructive criticism*. When you can recognize constructive criticism, it will make you twice as powerful and successful. You may already be doing well, but there may be things that someone else sees that will add a bit of refinement. Accept their comments graciously.

Keep adding more and more enhancing ingredients to your recipe to insure your emotional and physical vitality and spiritual strength are as best as can be. *Share* as much as you can. Be as much as you can to the people you love and care about. Live as well as you can. After you develop that hunger and thirst and zest for life, there's no turning back.

Sometimes in the late afternoon when the sun is setting, and I look out at the flow of traffic on our great interstate highway system with the television picking up the 5 o'clock world news via satellite and the telephone answering machine taking the calls and supper cooking in the microwave oven, I like to reflect on how much the world has changed over the past 50 years. Microcomputers, supersonic passenger planes, men walking on the moon, Israel and Egypt at peace, the collapse of communism, fax machines, video conferencing—these are just a few changes I've seen in my lifetime.

No turning back!

My parents lived at the beginning of this century and witnessed far greater changes even than I have. They saw the United States go from 38 to 50 states, saw the horse and buggy replaced by the automobile, saw rail travel replaced by airplane travel, saw the candle and the oil lamp give way to electricity in every home, and indoor plumbing and the telephone and radio and television.

It must have been like being born on one planet and, while completely wide awake and going about their daily business, being effortlessly transported by some friendly alien to an entirely different and strange world. They were born in an age of the telegraph and railroad and steamship, and they saw the birth of the atomic age.

Instead of fearing wild Indians, they learned that the entire human race could be wiped out by a single finger pushing the wrong button, but perhaps I am not giving my parents enough credit.

It's true they saw tremendous changes and the world of 1950 compared to the world at the start of the 20th century must have looked like a science fiction dream of the future come true, but not the way anybody would have predicted.

My parents not only lived with these changes, they managed to thrive with them. They brought electricity into their home and change into their lives. They grew with the times, they *welcomed the new*, they did not cling rigidly to the old ways, to the world they grew up with; rather, they were *flexible* and put down deep roots and flourished. They were not frightened or paralyzed by the terrible promise of the powers unlocked by atomic energy.

They believed in the good as well as in the terrible. They knew human nature and the will to survive. They often told me when I was a little boy not to be frightened by all the big claims made by people in the world because the human race was capable and adaptable and the will to survive was stronger than the will of anyone or the power of any machine.

A *strong character* is not a rigid character. In fact, exactly the opposite is true. Although it's important to be firm when you know something is right and to maintain that right position even when the crowd is going against you and wants to put you down, it's also important to remember that no person is God. Nobody is infallible or invincible.

Sometimes when the tide has run against you for a long time, it may be that what you held as a certainty was in fact not true in the light of overwhelming circumstances. It's not only right, it's also smart to be able to see more than one way to accomplish a task. It's wise to *see more than one solution* to any problem. It's a good skill to see things as someone else might see them because when the plan that served you so well for so long doesn't work anymore, then it's time to find another way. It's time to bend, it's time to move on, to change, to compromise, to talk—or you risk snapping like a dead branch in a stiff breeze. When it comes to lasting a long time, to standing tall and being strong, we must also *know when to bend*. Trees have a lot to teach us.

I've experienced firsthand the destructive power of a tropical storm. I witnessed close up and personal what a combination of wind and water can do to everything that stands in its path. The rain fell so long and hard that it completely soaked the ground and loosened the roots of even the tallest trees. At the same time, the wind blew with such force that century-old trees, tall and hard and strong, were blown over like toy soldiers standing on parade knocked down by a toddler at play.

However, enormous willows—standing tall as a house and covering an entire lot in some parts of the city—were bending and bowing gracefully to the slightest breeze and the mightiest gusts as each weathered the heavy blows of the storm.

They were almost the only large objects left standing after the air had cleared. Not only were tall trees and power poles and sea walls crushed by the storm, houses built to stand up under normal circumstances collapsed and their roofs were carried off in one piece and blown into the next county. Everything that tried to oppose the storm's fury was damaged or destroyed.

Everything that was *strong yet flexible* survived. When you were young, you may have played the game Rock, Scissors, Paper. In the game, scissors cut paper, paper covers stone, and stone breaks scissors. Whoever put out the winning fist symbol received a point. The best strategy was not to stick to the same symbol. You had to guess what your opponent would offer and turn your fist into what would defeat your opponent's scissors, stone, or paper.

This game teaches a child to think about the nature of materials, how something can be strong or appropriate in one situation—and yet be the wrong tool, a losing proposition, in another. It also teaches a child to vary approaches, to be flexible so that the opponent can't anticipate the next move. As you are trying to outsmart the other person, the other person is also trying to outsmart you.

THE NATURE OF CHANGE

It remains to be seen how the great changes we are seeing right now in our own day will affect our lives and the lives of our children and grandchildren. The nature of change is such that what today looks so large and important may turn out to be mere flashes in the historical pan. There may be something else we haven't even thought about. So no matter how much we prepare for one turn of fate, something will sneak up from the blind side when we're least expecting to be interrupted at our accustomed rounds. When that time comes, as it will, the people who survive and even triumph over the unanticipated will be people who are *ready to adapt*.

These people will bend in the first gust, they will step out of the path of the charging bull. They will pivot while holding their place in the scheme of things. They will step back and let something else bear the brunt of impact. I don't really think it's less important or more important today to *be open to change and flexible in adapting* to it than it has been in the past. It's always been important to be *flexible and farsighted,* anticipating whenever we can and, when we can't anticipate, being *prepared for all possibilities.*

The United States has been in existence for more than 200 years. Think of all the things that have happened in that time, the immense technological and social changes that have taken place. The founders deliberately left the Constitution a bit vague in some areas so that future generations would have the flexibility to adapt it to changing circumstances, and that's exactly what has worked—for more than two centuries.

FLEXIBILITY AND ADAPTABILITY

But now let's look back in time for a moment. The Roman Empire endured for about 500 years, more than twice the time the United States has existed. The framers of the Constitution closely studied the decline in fall of Rome to create an American government that would avoid a similar fate. So far, their efforts certainly seem successful, but it will be another few hundred years before we'll know.

And despite all the remarkable flexibility our form of government has displayed over the past two centuries, it's almost inconceivable that we will last as long as the ancient Egyptian empire that spanned more than 2,000 years. Famines, floods, invasions, and plagues came and went, but through it all there was an unbroken succession of Egyptian pharaohs. Nothing lasts that long without a great deal of flexibility.

Yet Egypt isn't even the all-time champion. The oldest and longest lasting empire in the world is that of the Chinese. How is this possible? It wasn't because of military power or tremendous wealth, because over the course of thousands of years those things came and went. Many times. The real reason the Chinese empire lasted so long was because of the work of two very different philosophers. The first, Confucius, provided ideas that became the solid foundation of the imperial government. Confucius taught a code of ethics that provided specific instruction on how the ruling classes could fulfill their duty to the nation and maintain law and order. He was essentially a lawgiver, a thinker who supplied fixed beacons for navigating the ship of state into the unknown future.

The second philosopher, Laozi, had a very different perspective. Historians associate Laozi's ideas with magic and with mystical powers, but he also placed a very modern kind of emphasis on the need for intuition and the ability to react quickly to change. Laozi pointed out that sometimes it is best to advance by retreating, that sometimes wars can be won by losing a few battles, and long-term goals can be achieved by accepting short-term reversals. By incorporating both perspectives, the ancient Chinese emperors developed a structure similar to that of modern buildings in Los Angeles and Tokyo that are built to withstand earthquakes. Their foundations are strongly reinforced, but there's also room for sway and give.

Flexibility is simple in theory, but tremendously challenging in practice. It means we have to learn to distinguish between what we can control and what is beyond our control.

Practicing flexibility requires great *self-knowledge* and iron *self-control* like a master of martial arts. To be flexible does not mean to be weak, to flounder about aimless and confused because we think there's nothing to be done. No, it requires *self-discipline*.

INNER FLEXIBILITY

Up to now, we've mostly talked about what might be called "tactical flexibility," where a specific situation requires knowledge of the various alternatives, and a specific set of circumstances requires nimbleness and dexterity.

More difficult and more important is the "inner flexibility" and long-range adaptability called for from the person who wants not just to survive, but succeed. A very wise man said, "You can't step in the same river twice." Every moment all things are changing, and the next minute is never like the last one. Whenever you achieve a hard-won success, it's always because you created a flexible response to the conflicting needs and ambitions and feelings of other people.

You've been able to sidestep the accidents of fate and the quirks of nature and your innate tendency. We all have to depend on yesterday's solutions to solve today's problems. I wrote about how the founders relied on Rome's example as they constructed the framework of American democracy. It's interesting to observe that at one of the times of greatest luxury and power and perhaps complacency ever in the history of the world, the heyday of the Roman Empire, a philosophy arose that attempted to teach these rulers of the known world how to govern themselves.

These philosophers called themselves Stoics and taught that to simply survive in life, let alone be a leader, you must learn to *take responsibility for the way things affect you.* At the same time, you must learn to bend with the wind of forces too great for your control. This kind of self-measurement and self-control should be part of every grownup's character. After all, an adult is the leader of the family, of the children who grow up in part learning from parental example to *be firm but fair, to be clear and consistent yet flexible* as signs of maturity.

TURN NOTHING INTO SOMETHING

The process of life change is not a matter of ability, it is merely a matter of will. Everyone can, but not everyone will. Decide right now to be one of the ones who will. Deliberately look at your life as a painter stands back and looks at the work of art on the canvas. Choose the area of your life where you know you need to touch up or start over. You can take steps to transform and bring everything together that we've discussed so far.

IMAGINE THE POSSIBILITIES.

First, to turn nothing into something, you start with ideas and imagination. How can we call ideas and imagination nothing? How tangible are ideas and imagination? It's a bit of a mystery. Yet, ideas can be turned into a hotel, into a business, into a vaccine; ideas can be turned into products and services to meet people's needs. Imaginations can turn into an entertainment park, a home, and a perfect vacation. You can't really call ideas and imaginations nothing. There must be some kind of substance to what ends up as something.

But we call it nothing because it isn't tangible—it isn't a hold-in-your-hand thing like a stick or stone. It isn't real, yet it is almost real. So to turn nothing into something, you start with ideas and imagination. Interesting. Ideas that become so powerful in your mind and your consciousness they seem real to you even before they become tangible. Imagination that is so strong that you can actually see it. When I built my first home for my family in Idaho all those years ago, before I started construction on this home, I took my friends and associates to the vacant property and gave them a tour through the house.

Is it possible to take someone on a tour through an imaginary house? The answer is yes. I used to say, "This is the three car garage." And the guy would look and say, "Yes, this garage will hold three cars." I could make it real, make it live. I would take them on a tour through the house. "Here's the fireplace that is brick on one side and stone on the other side. Here's the kitchen with this view out the window." And they would look out the "window" as I took them on the tour.

So the first step to making something out of nothing is to imagine the possibilities.

BELIEVE WHAT YOU IMAGINE IS POSSIBLE.

The second step of turning nothing into something is to believe that what you imagine is possible for you. And we become supported by testimonials that say something like, "Since I can do it, you can do it." And we start believing that— we have faith to believe.

We might also believe because of our own testimonial, "If I did it once, I could do it again. If it happened for me before, it could very well happen again." So we believe the testimonials of others who say, "If I can do it, you can do it. If I can change, you can change. If I can start with nothing, you can start with nothing. If I can turn it all around, you can turn it all around." And we also have the support of our own testimonial. "I accomplished something before, so I can do it again. I did it last year, I can do it again this year." Those two mindsets are very powerful. They're not actual substance, although they're very close.

Imagine that what's possible is possible for you—to have faith to believe. In fact, it's been written that faith is substance—*substance* meaning a piece of the real. Now, it's not the real, it's not rock, but it is so powerful that it's close to being real. It's written that "faith is the substance of things hoped for, the evidence of things not seen."[4] It's nothing in the sense that it can't be seen except with the inner eye. You can't hold it because it isn't yet tangible, but it is possible to turn nothing into something—especially ideas and imagination.

GO TO WORK AND MAKE IT REAL.

After you imagine the possibility and you believe it's possible for you, then you have to go to work and make that hotel, business, product, theme park, vacation, or whatever idea you imagined. Go to work and make a lifestyle of good health. Go to work and make a good marriage. Go to work and make it tangible, viable—breathe life into it and then construct it. Making something out of nothing is such a powerful ability for us as human beings.

Now here's the last ingredient for dramatic life change—*disciplined activity.* It takes disciplined activity to turn nothing into something. *Faith without activity serves no useful purpose, but faith invested into the activity creates reality.* Once I understood that, I knew then it was possible to build a career. I knew it was possible to build good health. I knew it was possible to build a relationship. I knew I could participate in the constructing of valuable things, valuable enterprises that would help and benefit other people.

Faith invested into activity creates reality.

I knew I could be part of it now that I understood that formula. Appreciate how disciplines turn imagination into reality—because without the disciplines, it doesn't work. The discipline to do the work is the last piece of the miracle process of navigating your future—to do the work of good health, to do the work of a relationship, to do the work of building the hotel.

NOTE

1. Hebrews 11:1 NKJV.

7

FINANCIAL INDEPENDENCE

After achieving financial success and being acknowledged as a wonder kid of success at age 31, I lost it all and went bankrupt. The lessons learned from that experience caused me to not only achieve greater success more quickly, but to sustain and grow my financial success throughout the rest of my life.

Everybody has to wrestle now with their own concept of financial independence or getting rich or becoming wealthy. I know some people are a little uncomfortable with those kinds of phrases, and I can understand that. We've heard the phrase that to love money would certainly be evil. But money's not evil. There are some evil ways to acquire it—which is the difference between greed and ambition. Contrary to the movie *Wall Street,* greed is not good. Greed is evil and must be dealt with. Greed hopes for something for nothing. Greed hopes for more than its share. Greed hopes for something at the expense of others. We call that evil. Greed is not good.

Here's what *is* good—ambition, legitimate ambition. Legitimate ambition says, *I only want something at the service of others, not at the expense of others.* Jesus gave the greatest scenario for success when He said, "Do you want to stand out?

Then step down. Be a servant. If you puff yourself up, you'll get the wind knocked out of you. But if you're content to simply be yourself, your life will count for plenty."[5]

Jesus gave the key to those who wish to be the greatest. He said, "The more lowly your service to others, the greater you are. To be the greatest, be a servant."[6] Service to many leads to greatness, not at the expense of many, not at the calamity of many.

The greed and lust for power caused Joseph Stalin, dictator of the Soviet Union (Russia) to kill 30 million of his own citizens. He gained power at the deadly expense of others, not at the service of others but by killing others.

Service to many leads to great wealth, service to many leads to great recognition, service to many leads to great satisfaction. These are facts of life.

Zig Ziglar probably said it as well as anybody, "If you help enough people get what they want, you can have everything you want." That's not greed; it's called legitimate ambition at the service of others. But I know some people who are struggling with this idea as we talk about how to get rich.

For years I've been teaching kids how to be rich by age 40, by 35 if they're extra bright, and much sooner if they find a unique opportunity. Some people are a little disturbed by my teaching kids how to get rich, teaching kids how to make a fortune. So I've modified it a little bit and here's the best I came up with—have the goal to become financially independent.

My definition of financial independence: *the ability to live from the income of your own personal resources*. It's powerful and a worthy goal. It's a legitimate ambition to render good service, to develop skills in the marketplace, and to become so valuable that you can have the resources you want. And finally have enough resources well invested so you can live independent from the income of your own personal resources. Then if you do wise things with your resources and the income, you can do all the things you want to do, support the projects you like, take care of things you always wanted to do. Financial independence is a worthy ambition to reach toward as you're navigating your future.

What you do with what you have is more important than what you have.

With that background, I recommend a book for you to read: *The Richest Man in Babylon* by George Clason. Perhaps you've already read it; I suggest you read it again. It's a small book; you can read it in one evening. I call it the appetizer for the full discourse on the subject of financial independence. The major theme of the book is that what you do with what you have is more important than what you have. What we do with what we have says so much about us. It reveals our philosophy of life, our attitude, what we know and what we think, and the makeup of our character. It's a reflection of what is going on inside our head and within our value system and decision-making process; what we do with what we have also reveals our ability to weigh experiences and to perceive opportunities.

The outer is always a reflection of the inner—it's an indication, a reading, a revealing. It speaks, it tells, it shows. Remember, everything is symptomatic of something—something right or something wrong. It is a wise policy not to ignore symptoms, for they can be early signs of a poor choice of philosophy or a sign that something important is being misread, misunderstood, miscalculated. So take a look at what you are doing with your money. What you're doing may be okay, all I'm suggesting is that you take a look.

Let me give you some of the details of a good financial plan as suggested by Clason's book. First, a very broad but important statement: *Learn to live on 70 percent of your net income.* "Net" meaning the money you have left after paying your taxes. The reason it's 70 percent is because you're going to be doing some very special things with the remaining 30 percent. So 70 percent is yours to spend.

Now let's talk about the all-important subject of how you allocate the 30 percent. I remember one day saying to Mr. Shoaff, "If I had more money, I would have a better plan." He said to me, "Mr. Rohn, I would suggest that if you had a better plan, you would have more money." So it's not the amount that counts, it's the plan that counts. It's not what you allocate, it's how you allocate it.

The first part of the allocation process of the 30 percent is 10 percent should go to charity. Give back part of what you have taken out to help those who cannot help themselves. I think that's a good percentage number, but of course you can pick your own percentage for charity (church, food bank, children's health care, etc.).

It's not the amount that counts, it's the plan and how you allocate it that counts.

It's your life and it's your plan, but giving your money to a church or to a charitable institution is a good idea. More often than not they know people in need. Whether you administer it yourself or give it to an institution to distribute, 10 percent should be given to charity. And by the way, the best time to teach this allocation process is when a child gets his first dollar. Take him on a visual tour. There's nothing better than visuals to illustrate what you're trying to teach. Take him to where some very unfortunate people live who cannot take care of themselves. Kids have big hearts. If they see the problem, they won't have any trouble giving a dime out of every dollar.

Here is what to do with the next 10 percent. Set it aside for capital (finances) you manage, find ways to utilize it, do some buying and selling yourself. Buy something, fix it, and sell it. Engage in commerce, even if it's only a part-time venture. Your home is a major capital project. In my opinion, we should all engage in capitalism in this country. We believe the people know what to do with their capital. They come up with ideas for goods and services brought to the marketplace. Capitalism is a dynamic enterprise that creates opportunities in abundance for people from all walks of life.

Now, here's the third allocation of the remaining 10 percent. Take 10 cents from every dollar and put it in a financial institution—into a savings account. This is a major benefit for all citizenry when you invest 10 percent of your earnings into the marketplace. Some projects in our society need more capital than one person can provide, so we have a system in which we can loan or invest our money so large businesses can be built to provide more jobs and products and services to help create an even more dynamic society.

Your money in a savings or investment account earns interest—you are paid for the use of your money. You can get back the money you loaned, and you'll have gained a profit for the use of your money.

And be sure to teach this to your kids; by the time they are 40 they will be wealthy enough to do what they want to do the rest of their lives, instead of all their lives doing what they have to do. Starting from your teenage years could take a much shorter period of time to become financially independent depending on what ideas and opportunities they take advantage of.

Mrs. Fields developed a new chocolate chip cookie and became a millionaire before she was 30. A 10-year-old takes a dollar, searches around the community, and finds a broken, abandoned wagon, pays a dollar for it, brings it home, cleans it up, sands off the rust, paints it till it's shiny and new, straightens out the wheel, and sells the like-new wagon for $11. You ask, does a 10-year-old deserve $10 profit? And the answer is, of course, society now has a mended wagon and that's what it's all about.

Find something and leave it better than you found it. Create value, build equity (value). It's how we build this most dynamic society called the United States of America, and everyone can contribute. Everyone can bring value to the marketplace. We can all be students of capital, profit, equity, and value. We can all engage in enterprise. We can all participate in the disciplines that bring wealth of lifestyle and treasure. All of us and our children can build the most powerful and attractive society ever.

We have the knowledge, the tools, the schools, the market, the resources. All we need is the will. Its riches are for the having.

Another part of financial independence is to *keep strict accounts*. This is the best of disciplines because too often we hear or say, "Where'd all the money go? It seems to just disappear." You have to have better discipline about keeping track of your funds. Know where and how much you have, always.

Next, I had to develop a *new attitude* as well as new concepts. I used to say, "I hate to pay my taxes."

Shoaff said to me, "Well, that's one way to live."

I thought, *Well, doesn't everybody hate to pay their taxes?*

As if hearing my thought he said, "No, a few of us have gone way past that mindset. Once you understand what taxes are, you realize that in our governmental system and our society, taxes are how you care and feed the goose that lays the golden eggs, which are democracy and liberty and freedom, free enterprise. Wouldn't you want to feed the goose that lays the golden eggs?"

Somebody may say, "Well, the goose eats too much." That's true, and I understand that. But better a fat goose than no goose. And the truth is, we all eat too much. Let not one appetite accuse another. Of course the government needs to go on a diet—so do most of us.

One of the classic stories of all time from ancient Bible scripts says that one day Jesus and His disciples were standing by the church treasury. Some people came by and put in big amounts. Some people came by and put in modest, average amounts. Then a little lady came by and put two pennies in the treasury.

In essence, Jesus says to His disciples, "Look, she gave more than everybody else. Her two pennies represented most of what she had, and if you give most of what you have then you've given the most." Wow, what a lesson to learn. It's not the amount, it's what it represents of your life that counts.

Now let me give you the wisdom of the scenario that did not occur, but may teach us one of the greatest pieces of wisdom taught in this scenario. Jesus did not reach into the treasury and get this little lady's two pennies and run after her saying, "Here little lady, My disciples and I have decided that you're so pitiful and you're so poor that we've decided to give you back your two pennies." I'm telling you that did not occur. If it would've occurred, it would've been what? Insulting.

She would've rightfully responded, "I know my two pennies aren't much, but it represents most of what I have. And would you insult me by not letting me contribute what I wanted to contribute even if it's only two pennies?" I'm telling you that did not occur. Here's part of the wisdom of the story that was not recorded—Jesus left her pennies in the treasury. Meaning everybody has to pay even if it's only pennies. That's the key.

And whether you start with pennies or whether you start with dollars or whether you start with nothing, remember, part of the scenario is to invest, and part of the scenario is to show a profit, and part of the scenario is to help take care of people who can't take care of themselves.

Set up your own philosophy. I'm not asking you to buy my philosophy; I'm not asking you to adopt my numbers. I only want to provoke you to think for yourself to come up with an economic philosophy that gets you thinking and pondering ways to use your resources and turn it into the dreams you want for the future.

To those who believe what Scripture says, "All things are possible." Nothing is impossible. The most incredible things are possible for believers—not hopers, believers. I'm telling you it's possible to multiply your income by 10 and then by 10 and then by 10. I lecture with General Norman Schwarz-kopf who receives $65,000 for one hour. I had lunch with Colin

Powell and was on a speaking panel for one of those multi-speaker seminars. He received about $70,000 for the seminar time. Unbelievable.

TWO DIFFERENT PHILOSOPHIES

There is a philosophy of the rich and a philosophy of the poor. First let's look at the philosophy of the poor. This is not meant to be demeaning; this is simply referring to people of modest means who tend to spend their money and invest what's left. If they have anything left over, they might save it or invest it. That's the poor philosophy, to spend your money, save what's left. On the other hand, the philosophy of the rich is to invest your money and spend what's left.

It's the same money, it's just a different attitude and a different philosophy. Either spend your money, save what's left—or invest your money, spend what's left.

When I was 25 years old, my mentor Mr. Shoaff said, "Show me your current financial plan for the future." And of course, I didn't have one.

He said, "Well, this would be a good time to lay out a good financial plan for the future, what to do with your money."

And I came up finally with the 70, 10, 10, and 10 formula. I don't spend more than 70 percent of my income; 10 percent is for church or charity; 10 percent is active capital, to buy and sell and make a profit; and 10 percent for passive capital (savings account)—let somebody else use your money, pay you interest, dividends, stock increase, whatever. It's a pretty good plan, 70, 10, 10 and 10.

A lady in Mexico one day said to me, "I heard your plan ten years ago. I followed it. I'm now a millionaire. I own two different properties because you also said, 'Don't buy the second car until you've bought the second house. Cars don't make you rich, real estate makes you rich.' I'm now about to buy the third house, so now I'm giving myself the luxury of buying the third car. I followed the 70, 10, 10, and 10 and taught it to other people. They're following it and getting great results."

WORK ON YOUR LIVING AND YOUR FORTUNE

One thing I didn't know when I was growing up and found out at age 25—I could work both on my living and my fortune at the same time if I had a good plan. Don't just work on your living, work on your fortune. Work on becoming financially independent.

Financial independence is the ability to live from the income of your personally invested resources. And the day you can finally do that is when you can work for joy and not necessity. And strangely enough, you probably work a lot harder for joy than you do for necessity.

I have a unique friend who started an enterprise. After about three years, he didn't have to work anymore the rest of his life. Now he's financially independent, but then he created a vast fortune in the next 20 years of his life simply because he was working for joy and not for necessity.

So get to that position as quickly as you can. The reason for earning a living is to make a fortune, not necessarily from your living but from what you earn invested wisely. A lady said to me, "Mr. Rohn, I'm in real estate."

I said, "Wonderful. How many properties do you own?"

She said, "No, no, I sell real estate."

I said, "Well, let me ask you one more time, how many properties do you own?"

Finally she got the message.

I said, "The reason for selling real estate is to earn the money to buy real estate. If you *sell* real estate, you make a living. If you *buy* real estate, you make a fortune."

INVESTMENTS

You may be wondering, *Should I invest conservatively or aggressively? What types of investments should I select? Should I invest when I have credit cards to pay off?* The whole world of financial options may seem unbearably complex. But resist this complexity by just picking a plan that feels right to you and, most importantly, get started.

First, you have to decide what your aversion to risk is—whether or not you can really tolerate it. I remember when those discoveries started coming out. If you paid off your home in 15 years instead of 30 by making one more payment a year, you saved more than the price of the house. Wow!

But some people really don't care as long as their payments are low; they will actually pay the extra price of the house just because the payments are low. And that's one philosophy, but it's not a good one. And if you have credit cards that charge interest rates more than 14 percent, paying them off and paying off your home in 15 years instead of 30 are very wise decisions. Why not save? Why not be prudent? Why not be careful? It's good practice even if you're wealthy. It's just good practice to be as practical as you can, not to be stingy and not to try to cheat anyone, but to do wise things with all your resources, especially financial.

The big challenge in life's adventure is the full development of all of your potential. The second big challenge is the wise use of all your resources, including your money and your time, which are two of the major resources—how to use your time and how to use your money.

If right now you're overwhelmed and in trouble with credit cards, I recommend you find someone who is knowledge-able and has a good strategy for rectifying the problem. There are some programs that can prevent collection people from harassing you. There are some programs that suggest bankruptcy. Rather than be pushed into bankruptcy, search for someone who will help you rearrange your whole financial landscape so you can start digging your way out. And once you start and begin making progress, you will definitely get excited about it. The numbers don't have to be huge and big as long as you're making progress. It feels great!

I firmly believe that your attitude and philosophy have far more to do with how wealthy you'll become than what you do for your profession.

So after you've dealt with your debt, you must wisely use the resources from your income to make a profit—even if you let other people use the money and pay you interest and div-idends. You can at least do that, whether you buy and sell or not. If you work on a job for 20 to 40 years, why couldn't you buy a piece of property and sell it for more than you paid for it? Why couldn't you buy a home and sell it for more than you paid for it?

Why couldn't you buy a piece of property that needs repair, find somebody to repair it, and sell it for more than you paid for it? Why couldn't you do that over the next some years as well as work on the job and punch the clock and do your duty and retire as a faithful employee? Why not work both on your fortune and your living? Why not?

If the least you did was to take part of what you earn as a living and let someone else use it and pay you for the use, you would easily be financially independent not from your job but from your investments. Then you can find other ways—it's stimulating and leads to other opportunities.

Arizona State University Professor Claude Olney developed a series for college students titled "Where There's a Will There's an A." He had attended one of my seminars years and years ago before he put that program together and he said, "I've got an idea. What do you think?" I said, "It's a winner!" Sure enough, it made him millions. He made money on every car he bought because of the incredible way he took care of it, and the way he made it shine and gleam so that when he got ready to sell it was worth more than when he bought it. That was just one of his projects. He also wrote a book of the same title that has helped countless people, especially students who need a bit more help.

Success all depends on your attitude and your philosophy. It's amazing. Two different people with two different attitudes: One lets opportunities go by the wayside because succeeding doesn't seem to matter much. Another one says, "I make the most of every opportunity to make money because it makes my life better."

AMBITION'S REWARDS

The economics of ambition, the rewards of ambition, the final result of working hard, burning the midnight oil, doing it until being disciplined to stay on track day after day, week after week, month after month—what's all this hard work get you? Better put—what's all this working smart going to get you? A life full of accomplishments, not only financial wealth, but you will be rich in everything that matters to you—family relationships, business dealings, spiritual and physical good health, mental acumen—whatever is important to you is yours.

As you have learned to set your goals and develop a game plan and use the tools of reflection and discipline in putting your life together, you're building your ambition to reach your destination as you set your sails toward your future.

Not only am I talking about the incredible feeling of accomplishment, I'm also referring to the tangible rewards of ambition. How wealthy should you be in knowledge and in spirit? As wealthy as you possibly can be. How rich should you be in dollars and investments? As rich as you possibly can be. I'm *not* talking about being greedy. I'm talking reward for success in the service of others, not at the expense of others. Is it okay to strive for success? Is it okay to strive to become rich and wealthy? Yes, when your attitude and motives are pure.

Many people struggle with the concept of being rich, thinking that rich people lack morals, rich people are cutthroat, rich people don't care. No, that's not true. Of course *some* rich people lack morals, are cutthroat, and don't care, but a lot of poor people have those same traits. Corruption is not inherent with being rich. Corruption is inherent with gaining wealth at the expense of others. Corruption is evil—wealth is not evil.

It's our natural destiny to grow, succeed, prosper, and find happiness.

Wealth says, *Discover your own talents and use them and take care of them so your own talents and skills and gifts can take care of you*. The more I ponder this topic of wealth, the more I firmly believe that it's our natural destiny to grow, to succeed, to prosper, and to find happiness.

Some people have the idea that to be wealthy or rich you have to misuse people, tell lies, and throw away values and integrity. If being rich bothers you, don't pursue riches. Some people even tell me that the Bible says, "It's hard for a rich man to reach heaven." Well, that language suits me. It doesn't say impossible, just hard. I don't mind a little hard stuff.

I'm also reminded that the Bible says the meek shall inherit the earth, but where does it say that in order to be meek you have to be poor? No, the Bible doesn't say you have to be poor. That's just an interpretation, a poor rationalization that lazy people use, people who need to justify their lack of progress, people who will give up in the midst of any adversity, people who don't even try. For everyone born in the United States of

America or who comes to America, part of your heritage is the opportunity to become financially independent.

HOPE AND PROMISE

In a nation full of hope and promise, it's our heritage and our right and within our reach to realize all the best that exists, including personal wealth. A man I know has an MBA from Harvard and an engineering degree from MIT. Smart guy, semi-retired now, and doing what he likes best—teaching. He teaches college courses in economics and business planning. When he teaches economics, he also teaches personal economics. And he starts his classes telling the students, "Decide how you want to live now versus how long you want to work. If you spend everything you make now, you'll have no choice but to work longer and harder. But if you start investing in your financial future now, you'll have the choice between retiring early, traveling more, continuing your career, or starting a new career later in life."

Think tomorrow, today—and live better tomorrow.

Once again, it all comes down to choices. Think tomorrow, today—and live better tomorrow.

Another point to remember when planning your economic future, if your business is high risk, if you're an entrepreneur whose career requires a great deal of risk and a great deal of strategic debt, keep the debt in your business and out of your personal life. I know this caution is hard because for most entrepreneurs looking for capital, the lender requires you guarantee the debt personally. So plan your debt just as you plan your fortune.

I urge you to take this fact seriously—*it's hard to get rich fast. It's easy to get rich slowly.* Think about the 70, 10, 10 and 10 formula, or whatever percentages you're working with. It doesn't happen overnight. With conservative investments, it takes a while. It takes discipline to keep adding value to your future, a little every month, a little every month, a little every month. It takes time to build your fortune, your financial independence. There's a saying about investing, "It takes time, not timing."

If playing the stock market is what you do, then you know that timing is a whole other ball game, but for the average person it's time. A study was done a while back that analyzed stock market investments. The study took two scenarios into consideration.The first took place over 40 years. In the first scenario, stocks were bought at the very worst possible time and sold at the very worst possible time. Bought high and sold low. And after 40 years the average return was around 10 percent. Scenario one dealt with time.

In the second scenario, stocks were analyzed over a 10-year period. The second scenario dealt with timing—stocks were purchased at the best possible time and sold at the best possible time. After 10 years, the average return was around 10 percent. Be patient in building your financial independence. It will come small steps at a time.

It's hard to be patient, but it's just like building your ambition and achieving your goals, it happens one step at a time. And what if patience has nothing to do with building financial independence? What about those "trust fund babies" who are handed their financial independence on a silver platter, never having to work a day in their lives? First car is a Porsche, first house is a mansion, first job is at daddy's company—what about those people born rich?

Someone says, "It isn't fair that I'm working like crazy all day, all week, all month, all my life. It just isn't fair. I'll never have that kind of money." Well, some things in life aren't fair. But what does that have to do with you, really? If your goal is to have greater financial independence, then start working harder and smarter on your goals, your own visions. And stop pondering what's fair and what isn't.

Work harder and smarter on your goals, your visions.

Unfortunately one of the disappointments that comes from your achievements is that there will be some people who don't aspire to do better. They will chastise and sometimes abandon you for your accomplishments, for your trying to become better. They may say, "What a friend—he's forgotten us now that he lives so well." And they'll probably say more than that. They'll gather in their little group and say unkind things to justify their own mediocrity.

But remember, those who choose to stay behind have chosen their own path, an average path, a path of mediocrity. And those who have climbed above the crowd almost always wish they could return to their earlier friends, to embrace them in friendship and love and try to help them get out of their ruts, to share ideas of hope and inspiration—but it rarely happens. Jealousy builds a big wall that is almost impossible to break down.

So as your life changes, your friends will change, your circle of influence will change. That's part of achievement and ambition and success—an ever-changing process required to become the person worthy of reaching your goals.

RISK

There are many reasons why people don't build their ambition, strive to become better, be the best they can. Many reasons, but it only takes one. We talked about fears earlier in the book and how to work to overcome them, but here's one we didn't talk about, *risk*.

The ambitions of an entrepreneur are different from the ambitions of an artist or a scientist or a teacher. With different levels of ambition come different levels of risk and different levels of reward. Salespeople are probably more able to handle risk than managers and professionals, and the higher the risk, the higher the earning potential. Entrepreneurs are probably even more risk-oriented. They have to be; an entrepreneur's ambition must overpower the risk of losing it all in an attempt to gain their dream.

Your level of ambition may or may not be equated with your ability to take on risk. Most people can't deal with so much failure to reach success. There are only a few people, even among the most ambitious, who have the tenacity, intestinal fortitude, and tolerance level to follow a risky ambition. Whatever the level of ambition, whatever the level of risk, there must always be the discipline to overcome the failures and see the end result.

So as you're developing your own plan for financial independence, as you're working toward the ideal of living off of 70 percent of what you make, remember the first step is to *define a plan*. It may not be ideal, but you're taking the first steps. And when you follow your plan:

- The money you put away today will help you build your financial independence tomorrow.

- And with financial independence, the result and reward of your ambition, comes freedom you've never known.

- Freedom and options to live where you want to live, do what you want to do, go where you want to go, drive what you want to drive, support the causes you want to support.

- With financial independence comes the freedom of choice.

It's okay to be rich. It's okay to be wealthy. It's okay to be successful as long as your motive is to help others—to be at the service of people, not at the expense of people.

NOTES

1. Matthew 23:11 *The Message*.

2. Matthew 23:11 The Living Bible.

8

TO LIVE WELL

This chapter title could also be "Lifestyle: Learning to Live Well." I truly believe in learning to savor and enjoy the fruits of great success; but not only that, I believe that the way you treated others and the unique way you live your life on the journey to success is just as vital. In this chapter you will see how living well can have a powerful impact on your family life, your friendships, and even your health.

Of all the parts of our life we want to work well, perhaps the most important is lifestyle. Mr. Shoaff gave me one of his strongest concepts when he said, "Don't just learn how to *earn*, learn how to *live*," and that's what lifestyle is all about. Learning how to live.

One of the great challenges of life is being happy with what you have while in pursuit of what you want. I have found this to be a practice well worth exercising with skill. Consider this. Some people have plenty of beautiful things filling their days, but they get little happiness from them. Some people have money, but they have trouble finding joy in their lives.

Imagine a father wads up a $20 bill and throws it at his son saying, "Here, if you need the darn stuff that bad, take it."

Same money, poor style. And remember, it's not the amount that counts, it's the style that counts.

Be happy with what you have while in pursuit of what you want.

Mr. Shoaff taught me about lifestyle in those early days, starting with small amounts. He said, "Imagine you're getting your shoes shined, and the shoe shiner has done a fabulous job. You have one of the world's all-time great shines, so you pay him for the shine. Now you consider from the change in your hand what kind of tip to give him, and the question pops into your mind. *Shall I give him one quarter or two quarters for my neat shine?* If two amounts for a tip ever comes to your mind, always go for the higher amount. Become a two-quarter person."

"What difference would that make? One quarter or two quarters?"

"All the difference in the world. If you choose to give him one quarter, that will affect you the rest of the day. You will start feeling bad. Sure enough, in the middle of the day you will look down at your great shoeshine and think, *I'm so cheap. One lousy quarter.* That will affect you. However, if you give the guy two quarters, the good feeling you have is almost overwhelming." That's lifestyle. Becoming a two-quarter person and receiving joy from the greater person you are becoming.

After speaking at a seminar in Saint Louis, Missouri, a man walked up and said, "Mr. Rohn, you really got to me. I'm going to change my philosophy. I'm going to change my attitude. I'm going to change my life. I'm going to change everything! You've touched me today. You'll hear about me, you'll hear my story someday."

I said, "Okay, great." Well, I knew that a lot of people say a lot of things.

But sure enough, a few months later I returned to Saint Louis to speak at another seminar. When I finished my seminar, I saw this man coming toward me. He said, "I'm sure you'll remember me as the man who said I was going to go make some changes—that you touched me with what you had to say. Well, I'm here to tell you that good things are already happening for me, in just a matter of months."

He said, "One of the things I decided to change was my relationship with my family. My wife and I have two lovely teenage daughters. Yet I give them trouble. Our daughters love to go to rock concerts and I always get on their case about it—the music is too loud and you're out too late. But they keep begging and when they beg long enough, I say, 'If you have to go that bad, just go,' and I shove the money at them. After I left your seminar, I decided to change all that, knowing it wasn't a lifestyle of living well."

The man continued, "Not long afterward, I picked up the newspaper and saw one of their favorite performers was coming to town. Guess what I did? I bought the tickets myself and brought them home, put them in an envelope, and later that day I handed them the envelope. I said to my two lovely daughters, 'You may not believe it, but inside this envelope are two tickets for the upcoming concert.' They couldn't believe it! And I told them, 'You'll be happy to know that your begging days are over.'"

He said, "I told the girls, 'Now, don't open the envelope until you get to the concert.' So they go to the concert, open the envelope, and hand the tickets to the usher. He says, 'Follow me.' And he starts walking down the aisle. The girls said, 'Hey, wait. Something's wrong, you're walking close to the front.' He looks at the tickets and says, 'No, nothing's wrong. Follow me.' They walked to the 10th row center. The only tickets they ever begged for was right third balcony. A little after midnight, my two daughters came bursting through the front door. One of them lands in my lap. The other one has her arms around my neck. They're both saying, 'You're one of the all-time world's great fathers!'"

He was beaming and said, "Mr. Rohn, you're right. I can't believe it—same money, different father, different style. I started making the changes and started with my teenagers, my girls. What a difference the changes are making in my life and our family lifestyle."

DEVELOP A BETTER LIFESTYLE

You can improve your family and relationship lifestyles too. You can do it with your sales or management career. You can do it with your friendships. You can do it with any part of your life. Don't curse what you have, don't complain about what you have—the seed, soil, sunshine, rain, miracles, and seasons—start changing and processing and evaluating your lifestyle today and this process of change will become a wonderful routine. You will be amazed at what can happen in such a short period of time.

So develop your lifestyle—include a style of seeing, giving, sharing, enjoying. It's not the amount that counts, but the experience of choosing to live with style.

I remember saying to Mr. Shoaff, "If I had more money, I would be happy."

And he gave me some of the better words of wisdom when he responded, "Mr. Rohn, the key to happiness is not *more*. Happiness is an art to be studied and practiced. More money will only make you more of what you already are. More will only more quickly send you on to your destination. If you're inclined to be unhappy, if you get a lot of money, you will be miserable. More money will only make you more. More money will only amplify what you already are. If you are inclined to be mean and you get a lot of money, you will be a terror. If you are inclined to drink a little too much, when you get a lot of money, you can now become a drunk."

So style is not more. Style is an art, a genius, a design. Lifestyle is reserved for those who are willing to study and practice the higher arts of life. Lifestyle is culture, music, dance, art, sculpture, literature, plays, concerts. *Lifestyle is a taste of the fine, the better, the best.* Philosopher Mortimer Adler says, "If we don't go for the higher tastes, we will settle for the lower ones." So develop an appreciation for the fine. That is a worthy purpose—developing an appetite for the unique things in life. Study the art and reach for the best. To have the best in the time we have available to us, that is the quest. Remember, it's not the amount, it's the imagination.

STYLE COUNTS

My lady and I were on a trip to Carmel, California one sunny summer day to do some shopping and exploring. I stopped to have the car serviced at a gas station. A young man, about 18 or 19, came bouncing out to the car with a big smile and said, "Can I help you?" I said, "Yes, a full tank of gas, please." Well, not only did he fill the tank with gas, he checked every tire, washed every window, even the moon roof, checked everything—and all the time he was working, he was whistling and singing.

We couldn't believe all the service and his obvious happiness. The young man brought me the bill and as I was signing it, I said, "Hey, you really have taken good care of us. I appreciate it." And he said, "I really enjoy working. It's fun for me. I get to meet nice people like you." We couldn't believe it. This kid was so sincere.

I said, "My lady and I are going to Carmel and we want to drink one of those $2 milkshakes on the way up there. Where is the nearest Baskin-Robbins?"

He said, "That's a great idea. Baskin-Robbins is just a few blocks away." And he told us where to find it and he said,

"Don't park out front. Park around to the side so your car won't get hit."

What a kid. So we drove to Baskin-Robbins, walked in, checked the flavor board, and ordered milkshakes. However, instead of ordering two milkshakes, we ordered three. Then we drove back to the station. The young kid dashed out to the car again and said, "Hey, I see you got your milkshakes."

I said, "Yes, and this one is for you." When I offered it to him through the window, he couldn't believe it.

He said, "For me?" I said, "Sure. With all the fantastic service you gave us, I couldn't leave you out of the milkshake deal."

He said, "Wow, no one has ever bought me a milkshake."

I said, "Have a nice day." Then I buzzed up the window and we drove away. When I looked in the rearview mirror, there he was, holding that milkshake, a big surprised smile on his face. Now what did that cost me? Only $2. Hey, I've enjoyed and shared the memory of that experience 100 times. For just $2. Remember, it's not the amount that counts, it's the style.

That same day, I guess I was feeling extra creative. When we got to Carmel, I drove straight to the flower shop. We walked inside and I said to the florist, "I need a long stem red rose for my lady to carry while we go shopping around Carmel." She was impressed. The florist said, "Well, we sell them by the dozen."

I said, "I don't need a dozen, I just need one."

He said, "That'll cost you a couple of dollars for just one."

I said, "Wonderful. There's nothing worse than a cheap rose." I selected the rose, handed it to my lady and said, "Here, carry this while we stroll around town." She was impressed, and the cost? Just $2.

A couple of hours later we were having some refreshments and my lady looked across the table and said, "Jim, I just thought of something. I think I'm the only lady in Carmel today carrying a rose." For $2. Can you imagine the joy that $2 brought to her that day? Remember, it's not the amount.

Live your life in style.

Just two ideas and a total cost of $4 for unique experiences and sweet memories. Just two modest examples of how easy it is to put style in your life. Make sure you don't miss out. Don't miss anything you can enjoy. Be sure you live your life in style.

LIFE AND BALANCE

One last major point—life and style is also life and balance. Make sure you pay attention to all the values and dimensions of your life. One is family—when you have someone you care about, that's a priceless gift. One person caring for another is life in the best of style and value. Protect it with a vengeance. If a chair gets in the way, I suggest you destroy the chair.

It was wisely said so long ago, but is still true for today: "There are many treasures, but the greatest of these is love." Better to live in a tent on the beach and have a love affair than to live in a mansion by yourself. Ask me. I know. Family must be cultivated like an enterprise, like a garden. Time and effort in imagination, creativity, and genius must be summoned constantly to keep it flourishing and growing.

FRIENDS

After family is friendship; friendship is a valuable treasure. Friends are those incredible people who know all about you and still like you. Friends are people who are coming in when everyone else is leaving. And as someone once suggested, be sure to make the kind of friends on your way up who will take you in on your way down. Life is a bit of both up and down, but with true friends, friends who care regardless of your circumstances, the ups are more automatic and the downs less devastating.

I have one very special friend, though. If I was stuck in a Mexican jail and accused unduly, I would call this friend. Guess why I'd call this friend? He would come and get me. Now that is a friend, someone who would come and get you no matter what.

I also have some casual friends who would probably say, "Call me when you get back." I guess we all have some of those friends.

167

Friendship is vitally important to those who want to live well. Make sure your friendships get the attention and the effort they deserve. Properly nourished, friends will give back to you that priceless treasure of both pleasure and satisfaction called the good life. And remember, living well is not an amount. The good life is an attitude, an act, an idea, a discovery, a search. The good life comes from a lifestyle that is fully developed regardless of your bank account so that it provides you with a constant sense of joy in living and fuels the fires of commitment to all of the disciplines and fundamentals that make life worthwhile.

What is wealth without character, industry without art, quantity without quality, enterprise without satisfaction, possessions without joy? Become a person of culture to add to the whole culture for we are most certainly a product of all the values of our community and country. Become that person of unusual substance who brings an added measure of genius to the whole so that our children and the children of many will be the beneficiaries of the treasure.

Invest in your life.

I encourage you to make a list of the 20 most important people in your life. Then note how long it's been since you've communicated with each one. Like me, you probably have listed some people you consider very close friends, yet you haven't spoken or written to them in a very long time. To keep friendships alive, we have to pay more attention and take time to reach out. Make a phone call. Set a lunch date. Drop in on a nearby friend.

Staying in touch is just as vitally important as developing a good relationship. Take care of what and who matters. If nobody calls me on my birthday, that doesn't matter to me. But for someone else, it does matter. Keep track of those kinds of things. It's easy to lose track of the details in our busy world, it's easy to let things slide, but we later have regrets that we didn't stay in touch more often, especially somebody older who passes. Do what it takes to keep a good relationship going. It's like tending a garden.

Investing life into life has the potential to create miracles. Investing life into life with ideas, information, association, influence, and enterprise can create a corporation, business, movement, something that benefits many more people than just those few who might invest in each other's lives.

Be valuable enough to invest in somebody else's life.

So that should be one of your goals—to be valuable enough to invest in somebody else's life, starting first with your children, if you're married, and then invest in each other. Marriage and friendships are opportunities to invest in each other's personal lives.

You and a business associate can take advantage of opportunities to invest in each other's life, which can affect a lot of other people's lives. Bill Bailey and I continued to invest in each other for years. I would come up with a great idea so I called him. He comes up with a book he's read, and he calls me to say, "This is a masterpiece. You've got to read it." We invest in each other in many different ways to benefit both of us. What I share with him, he shares with others, and what he shares with me, I share with you and others around the world. That contribution of sharing with each other, being influential, providing leadership, and contributing to someone's life can continue indefinitely.

Friendship is one of the most valuable possessions in the world. Good friends, relationships. What really matters when we get right down to it is our inner circle. We should spend as much time as possible, maximum time, with family, our inner circle, and close friends. Maybe borrow a little from other things that that are essential but not quite that valuable.

Because that's where a lot of the drive and ambition to do well comes from. Making dreams come true for your inner circle furnishes the fuel for high ambition. Not to be ambitious just for the name or fame or money or for being generous in the future, but at least to do as much as you can to nourish that association and communication in your inner circle.

Conversations can be a form of art. Years ago we wrote letters that were sent or received once in a while. Now we just pick up the phone (or send a text or email). But back then people took thoughtful care about putting into words how they really felt. Now it's too easy to be too quick and casual in our communication—people don't really care about the language, especially when we're talking (or texting) 24 hours a day. It's hard to be unique, to say something extraordinary about how we feel, because it gets lost in the nonstop, mundane, ordinary conversation.

When Judy, my wife, and I parted ways, I wrote a little note, "Dear Judy, as often as the night comes, so does my sadness. As constant as the day arrives, so is my love for you. I wish for you and I wish the best for you. And I understand that dilemma. My life is here where you touched me. If ever you should call, I will be there to be touched again." I took a little time to thoughtfully see if I could say in a very few words what was happening to me at the time. It's easy to be careless with language and not say what you mean to get a point across.

I want to be well-read and have good command of language and be able to translate my own feelings and experiences into useful conversations so that when the need arises, I'll have something valuable and wise to say, however short or long it may be.

It's like fishing. You can't jerk too hard or you lose them and you can't leave too much slack. Let them off the line, they're gone. So it's called pull, pull, pull. Easy, easy, pull, pull, easy, easy, to learn how to fish, to catch fish.

It's similar with communication. Strong enough but not too strong. It can't be weak or the point doesn't get across. It has to be strong. Strong without being rude. Well-chosen words mixed with measured emotion, not too much, not too little. When the actor gives a performance, if the script is well-written, that's part of the structure. The rest is delivery. Part of it is style, but part of it is enough emotion for the point, not too much, and I think parents have to do the same.

How do you put both strong feelings, love and hate, in the same sentence? We have to do it because we have to deal with both. What's right, what's wrong, what's better, what's okay, what would be better? We all struggle with language. Words are clumsy sometimes when you try to express what's going on in your head, let alone your heart.

It's not an easy challenge, but it's how you build empires. It's how you create great societies. It's how you share the intricacies of philosophy that can change somebody's life. And whether you have a unique rational conversation with a child, a son or a daughter, or whether a president has a rational conversation with the country, you try to make it unique as you can to get the point across.

If you're married and you have children, I have great advice for you. Here's the best I can give you. I'm not a counselor, but this is great stuff. Here's number one—if the parents are okay, the kids are okay. Your own self-development is the best contribution you can give to your children—not self-sacrifice, self-development and contribution. Self-sacrifice usually earns contempt. Self-development and self-investment earn respect. A friend coined the phrase that I like: "I'll take care of me for you, if you'll take care of you for me."

Likewise, the best contribution I can make to you, if you're my friend, is my personal development. What if I become 10 times wiser, 10 times stronger, 10 times better, 10 times more unique? Think of what that will do for our friendship.

The best contribution to your company is your self-development. The best contribution to your husband or your wife is your personal development to become all you can become, as wise as you can and as kind as you can and as unique as you can.

Accept the pain but not the guilt.

An added piece of advice: In whatever decisions you have to make, if you've made the best decision possible but it's going to cause some pain, you must learn to accept the pain but not the guilt. There's a part of us that tries to make us feel guilty if we made a painful decision that affected other people, yet it had to be made. So a key to maintaining good mental health is to accept the pain but not the guilt—because it's not pain that destroys you, it's guilt.

RIGHT THINKING AND RIGHT LIVING

Good health is the direct result of right thinking and right living. In other words, good health is the direct result of strong character.

Case in point. A buddy told me about his former football coach who always told the boys on the team that the most important thing they could do for themselves—as a team playing football *and* as individuals playing the game of life—was to develop what he referred to as a "healthy attitude." Sure they had to do push-ups. They had to tackle a dummy and push the blocking sled, but if they didn't do it with a healthy attitude, then as far as this seasoned coach was concerned, they were just dead weight pushing around more dead weight.

They were all young and strong physically, but the coach emphasized a healthy attitude, which has to do with character. Being in good health raises your esteem, your standing, and even respect from other people. Good health may give your character and ambition every advantage and put you in the way of the good things in life that come along.

But to all these benefits of good health, there is even more. Despite the great and certain worldly rewards for staying healthy and fit, they are not the only or even the main reason to seek and embrace the habits of good health.

If I can be allowed a moment of philosophical reflection—the greatest benefits to health are found in the mind and spirit and soul of the seeker. *Hold on a minute,* you're thinking, *are you going to go all fuzzy and mystical?* No, I'm talking sense, not preaching or pushing vitamins.

In fact, if I knew the answer to what the true path to good health is, I would hold the key to the most vexing problem of the ages. And this book would be the basis of a religion, not a practical guide to navigating your future toward achieving success. Good health may really be an effective character trait as much as a cause of it. In my opinion, being a person of strong character is the best prescription for a sound mind and a sound body.

If you feel good about yourself, you'll naturally want to take care of your body; but if you lose respect for your body, you are more likely to become slipshod in other areas too. Older people are probably the strongest people in the world; because if they weren't, they wouldn't have lived so long.

Having a strong character is the best prescription for a sound mind and a sound body.

COMMON SENSE TIPS FOR GOOD HEALTH

There are certain foods that help the plumbing work smoothly, help with digestion. But those foods alone don't make for a healthy and balanced diet. Ensure you *have a variety in your diet* to fulfill your body's many nutritional needs.

What's true of financial health is also true of physical well-being. If you keep doing exactly what you've been doing, you will continue to have exactly what you have. Anybody who does the same thing every day, year in and year out with no break or vacation, is probably in no position to even know whether he or she is in good shape. Take care of yourself by *frequently stepping out of your routine*.

As discussed earlier, you can't know what you have until you leave it or lose it or get something else. Probably the easiest and most helpful way to break up your day and keep the biological clock wound up so that it doesn't run down in the middle of the best days of your life is to *catch a nap* whenever the opportunity presents itself.

But I stopped taking naps when I graduated from kindergarten, you may object. And I ask you, have you been better off because of that? What does every chief executive officer of any major corporation have in the office right there across from the big desk with its leather upholstered, tilted back, swivel chair? A couch. And what do you suppose that couch is for? For a little snooze before addressing the board about the latest attempt at a hostile takeover or the upcoming stock-holders meeting.

Remember, every dream is a vacation, and it was Shakespeare who said that "Sleep knits up the raveled sleeve of care." President John Kennedy kept to his scheduled naps even during the Cuban Missile Crisis in 1962. Did this save the world from nuclear catastrophe? Well, something saved it.

Mens sana in corpore sano means "A sound mind in a sound body." It's a Latin saying, and the ancient Roman prescription for living the good life, smart life, and feeling good and smart about yourself. You just can't sharpen your mind like a pencil so it comes to a fine point—and gets shorter and shorter until it's worn down to a stub and has to be discarded. Neither can you just eat and drink and party and fight as if without a care in the world—or so the Romans believed during their glory days. I agree with that line of thinking. Later in the declining days of the empire, the Romans forgot their own advice, and soon the decline became a fall. I'm sure the message is clear.

For centuries, the people of China have absorbed wave upon wave of conquering barbarians into the vast reaches of their country. Always the invaders seize control of the government. But then a curious thing happens and has happened every time to the conquering hoards. After a few years of rule, the Chinese don't become barbarians, but the barbarians become Chinese.

Part of the reason for this ability of the Chinese people to swallow up and digest the armies that would rule them has to do with the country being so large. Another part of it has to do with the philosophy and practical wisdom of this mighty nation, which has for many thousands of years made a science of good health and long life. It's the national character, we might say.

One form of the martial arts that centers on self-defense, an art called Tai Chi, combines physical exercises with philosophy and diet. It teaches people to defend themselves from all

177

kinds of attacks—attacks from hostile people using weapons or surprise or brute strength, attacks from within the physical body in the form of disease, and even attacks in the form of destructive emotions like anger or fear.

Character and chemistry are both taken into account. I'm not touting mysticism; I'm just following my philosophy of learning things wherever I can. I've heard of a very old Chinese man who lived an odd but astonishing long life. He ate very little, exercised regularly, and kept a turtle in his bathtub. The turtle, he explained, was a symbol of longevity and it gave him an example to follow in his dealing with the world, slow and steady, and it supplied a certain kind of undemanding companionship in what must have been at times a lonely life.

Good health is an aspect of character— ethical people are happier and relaxed.

There's much more to be said about health, but there are few hard and fast conclusions to be reached. I think health is an aspect of character because I see evidence that ethical people are happier and more relaxed. Stress on the other hand, which I associate with hostility and anger, is said to cause physical problems. But maybe this is just wishful thinking, that people get what they really deserve. I happen to believe they do get what they deserve, however—or perhaps they get even a little bit more.

There's really no end to talking about health and living well. Good health is about going on, about continuing for as long as you can. It's not about stopping, quitting, and giving up. What's healthy is persisting as far and as long as you can. Maybe speeding up or pausing along the way, maybe even taking a side path instead of staying on the beaten path.

Staying healthy is the only way to live well in all the parts of life. It's the way you stay strong and the way you stay interested. It's where the mind and body meet. And in a sense, good health is what all the hard work is about. It's why the heart and the mind and the muscle cooperate.

9

LIVING THE GOOD LIFE

In this concluding chapter, I share with you my short list to the good life—to happiness and success. There are also four questions for you to consider as you begin your journey to success.

My short list to living the good life:

1. **Productivity.** If you don't produce, you won't be happy. Make a conscious effort to be productive every day in some way.

2. **Good friends.** The greatest support system in the world is good friends. You have to work on creating that system and then take time to maintain it. Don't be careless. Friends are those wonderful people who know all about you and still like you.

3. **Spirituality.** I'm not asking you to be a believer. I believe that humans are more than an advanced form of the animal kingdom. I'm a believer that humans are a special creation. I don't ask you to be a believer, but here's what I do ask. If you are a believer, study, practice, and teach. Why? It builds

the foundation that builds the family, the schools, churches, and the country that builds the nation, that helps us to compete among the nations of the world.

4. **Don't miss anything.** Don't miss the game, the performance, the movie. Don't miss the words, the music. Elton John sang, "She lived her life like a candle in the wind, never knowing who to cling to when the rain set in." Don't miss the songs that nourish the soul. You can't describe how brief and fragile life is much better than that. Winston Churchill wrote in his *War Memoirs* book, "Truth is incontrovertible. Panic may resent it. Ignorance may deride it. Malice may distort it. But there it is." Don't miss the words. Feast on someone else's wisdom. Do your research. It's part of living a good life. Why? It'll serve you well forever. If you live well, you will earn well. If you live well, it shows in the texture of your voice. If you live well, it shows up on your face. If you live well, it shows in the magnetism of your personality. If you live well. So don't miss the nourishment of all the things around you that may help you live a good life.

5. **Your inner circle.** Take care of them. They'll take care of you. Inspire them. They will inspire you. Not much of anything else is more valuable than your inner circle. That's where the power to conquer the world comes from. When a father walks out of the house and he can still all day feel his daughter's kiss on his cheek, he's a powerful man. The nourishment of the inner circle is so incredible. When a spouse

can still feel the love of the other throughout the day, that motivation carries for a long time. One person caring for another is the greatest of virtues. There are many virtues and values, but the greatest is love.

6. **Ask for God's help.** We can all use a little help. This entire book is about what you can do to navigate toward a successful and fulfilling future. Yet, I still recommend God's help along the way. He's always available and willing to share His wisdom with you. Consider this story: A man took a rock pile, turned it into a fabulous garden. Someone walked by and saw it and said, "You know, you and the good Lord have made a fabulous garden here." The gardener said, "I understand your point, but you should have seen it a few years ago when God had it all by Himself." So we do play a part.

In addition to the short list, the following five abilities should also be part of your personal development quest to live the good life:

1. DEVELOP THE ABILITY TO ABSORB.

The ability to soak it up like you're doing right now as you're reading. Be a sponge soaking up everything, not just the words but also what you're feeling and thinking. Don't miss the scenarios I've written about and the atmosphere they created in your mind. Most people just try to get through the day. But I want you to commit to learning something from each day. Don't just get through it, let the day teach you. Join the university of life. What a difference that'll make in your future. Commit yourself to learning and absorbing.

I have a personal friend who's gifted in this area. He has soaked up and remembers everything that has ever happened to him. He can tell you as a teenager where he was and what he did and what he said and what she said and how they felt and the color of the sky and what was going on that day. He gets it. It's more exciting to have him go to Acapulco, come back, and tell me about it than it is to go myself. He is unbelievable; he doesn't miss a thing. Here's a good phrase to jot down—*Wherever you are, be there, absorb it all, capture it in your mind's eye*. Take a picture if you can, but also let your soul and heart take pictures. This is such an important ability to develop—be deliberate about the ability to get it. Key phrase: *casualness leads to casualties*.

2. LEARN TO RESPOND.

The ability to respond means let life touch you—but don't let it kill you. Let sad things make you sad. Let happy things make you happy. Give in to the emotion. Let the emotion strike you. Not just the words, not just the image. Let the feeling strike you. Let the emotions strike you. It's important that our emotions are as educated as our intellect. It's important to know how to feel, how to respond. It's important to let life in, let it touch you.

I'm the greatest guy in the world to take to the movies. I get into a good movie. Make me laugh, make me cry. Scare me to death. Teach me something. Take me high, take me low. Just don't leave me as I was when I came in.

I picked up a newspaper in Australia and the advertisement read, "See Dr. Zhivago on the big screen." I'd seen it two or three times before, but not on a big screen. So I went one more time; and sure enough, I was swept away again by the story of the Russian Revolution, Dr. Zhivago, and that whole scenario.

I had previously missed the importance of the ending of that movie, but this time I got it. Comrade General was talking to Tonya, asking, "How did you come to be lost?" She said, "Well, the city was on fire and we were running to escape and I was lost." He pressed her again. "How did you come to be lost?" And she said, "Well, while we were running through the city and it was on fire, my father let go of my hand and I was lost." That's what she didn't want to say.

Comrade General said, "Tonya, that's what I've been trying to tell you. Comarovsky was not your real father. He was not. I've been looking all over for you. This man, my relative, Dr. Zhivago, the poet. *He* was your father. Tonya, if this man, your real father, had been there with you, I promise you he would have never let go of your hand."

And this time I got it. The other times I was eating popcorn, waiting for the movie to finish, whatever. I'm asking you to get it, get life—absorb and respond to it. Pay attention. Pick up life's colors, sounds, and what's going on.

3. DEVELOP THE ABILITY TO REFLECT.

Reflect means go back over, study again. Go back over the notes you've made in this book. Read the text one more time. In addition, each evening, I encourage you to reflect over your day so that the important aspects of the day lock firmly in your mind. Who did you see, what was the conversation? How did you feel? What happened? Capture each day as a piece of the mosaic of your life. Lock in the experience—the knowledge, sights, sounds, the panoramic color motion picture of the day. It will serve you for the future.

It's important to learn how to reflect with yourself. There's something to be said for solitude, for taking occasions to shut out everything else for a while. I head for the mountains and ride the Jeep trails where there are very few human beings. Or I go out in the desert somewhere. This is my time to get away. When you live a very public life, you treasure solitude. A chance to reflect, go back over past experiences, skills, schedule, etc. There are some things you need to do alone—ponder, think, wonder, read, study, absorb, soak in. See if you can become better this year than you were last year—better the next five than you were the first five.

Why is it important to reflect? To make the past more valuable to serve you for the future. Learning to gather up the past and invest it in the future is really powerful. Gather up today and invest it in tomorrow. Gather up this week and invest it in the next week. Gather up this year and invest it in the next year. That's so powerful. Rather than just hanging in there one more year, see what's going to happen.

Learn, study. This is part of the personal development quest—becoming better than you are, more valuable than you are. Not just in terms of economics, in terms of motherhood, in terms of fatherhood, in terms of being a better brother or sister, better colleague, making a better contribution to the family, to society, to the community, to the church, to the office, to the commitment, to the partnership.

It doesn't matter what it is that has value. Work on yourself. Then you bring more value to the partnership, to the marriage, to the franchise, to the corporation, to the enterprise, to the community, to the nation. That's self-development, personal development. The best contribution you can make to someone else is self-development. Not self-sacrifice. Self-sacrifice only earns contempt. Self-development earns respect.

4. DEVELOP THE ABILITY TO ACT.

Take action—not hastily, unless required. Don't lose time trying to figure out all the tiny details. The time to act is when the idea's hot and the emotion is strong. If you would like to have a library like mine, if you feel strongly about that, go buy that first book, and then get a second book. Before the feeling passes and before the idea gets dim, take action pronto, immediately. Do something as soon as possible.

If you don't, we call it *the law of diminishing intent*. We *intend to* follow through when the idea strikes and the emotion is high. But if you don't translate that into action fairly soon, the intent starts to diminish, diminish, diminish. And a month from now, it's cold. A year from now, it can't be found. So act. Set up a discipline when the emotions are high and the idea is strong and clear and powerful. That's the time to set up the discipline.

Somebody talks about good health and you're stirred: "Right, I need to get a book on nutrition." Get the book before the idea passes and before the emotion gets cold. Go for the book, start the library, start the process. Fall on the floor, do some push-ups. Action. You must take action. Otherwise, the wisdom is wasted and the emotion soon passes—unless you put it into a disciplined activity. Capture it.

THE GREATNESS OF DISCIPLINE

Discipline is how to capture the emotion and the wisdom and translate it into equity. All disciplines affect each other. In fact, here's a good philosophical phrase—everything affects everything else. Nothing stands alone. Don't be naïve thinking, *Well, this and that don't matter.* I'm telling you *everything matters.* There are some things that matter more than others, but there isn't anything that doesn't matter.

Every let-down affects the rest. This is part of the educational process on personal development. If you don't take the walk around the block, you probably won't do the apple a day. If you don't do the apple a day, you probably won't start building your library. If you don't build your library, you probably won't keep a journal, and you won't take pictures. You won't do wise things with your money or your time, and you won't do wise things with your possibilities and relationships. And very quickly, six years of "don'ts" accumulate and you know you messed up. The key to reversing that process is to start absorbing disciplines into your lifestyle.

The positive side—every new discipline affects the rest of your disciplines. That's why action is so important. The least action, the smallest action—take it. When you start accomplishing and the value starts to return from that one action, it'll inspire you to do the next one and the next one and the next one.

When you start walking around the block, you will be inspired to eat an apple, which will inspire you to read a book, and then you'll start writing in a journal, which will inspire you to grow and develop necessary skills. All positive disciplines affect all the others. Every negative or lack of disciplines affects the rest. The key is to diminish the lack and increase the positive—and voila! you've started a whole new life process.

Discipline's greatest value is the sense of self-worth and self-esteem it gives you.

One more thought on discipline. The greatest value of discipline is the sense of self-worth and self-esteem it gives you. Self-esteem is directly connected to your disciplines. The least lack of discipline will start to erode your psyche. The slightest lack of doing your best will cause a subtle but constant diminishing of your self-worth, self-confidence, and self-value.

Instead of doing your best, you do just a little less than your best, thinking, *Well, it's only going to affect my sales.* No, it's going to affect your consciousness and your philosophy too.

189

The problem with "the least neglect" is that it starts as an infection and then becomes a disease if you allow it.

So, how can you regain your self-respect after sliding backward? All you have to do is start the smallest discipline that corresponds to your philosophy. Think: *I should..., and I could..., and I will. No longer will I let neglect stack up on me. I don't want this same sorry scenario six years from now, giving some sorry excuse instead of celebrating my progress.* That's the key to discipline.

I suggest you get your kids involved in disciplines. One more and then one more, and the first thing you know, you're starting to weave the tapestry of a disciplined life into which you can pour more wisdom and more good attitude and more strong feeling, more faith, and more courage. Now the equities start to flow. And if you start this process in your children early in life, the positive return will be very exciting—for them and you! You will commit yourself to this strategy for the rest of your life.

You can transform your life spiritually, socially, personally, economically, and every other way. You can be rich and powerful and sophisticated and healthy and influential. Don't let somebody sweep you into some way contrary to nature itself. The miracle of the seed and the soil and the seasons and God and all that's available, sunshine and rain, is only available to you by labor, so labor well.

DO THE BEST YOU CAN

Now here's the last advice on discipline—*do the best you can.* Question: Is the *best* you can do *all* you can do? Answer: No. Strangely enough.

If you fell on the floor right now and did as many push-ups as you possibly could, and the best you can do is five, anyone looking at your red, sweaty face would probably say that's true. Five is the *best* you can do.

Now is five *all* you can do? The answer is no.

If you rest a little, you can do five more. And if you rest a little, you can do five more. And if you rest a little, you can do 15 more. How did we get from five to 15? It's a miracle. And if you rest a little, you can do 15. Rest a little, you can do 20. How did you get from five to 20? It's a miracle. Did you know you can keep doing that? Do a little more, rest a little, do a little more, rest a little, and finally get up to 50 push-ups.

Is it possible to get up to 50 push-ups? Of course.

Here's the clue: Make rest a necessity, not an objective. The objective of life is not to rest. The objective of life is to act. Think of more disciplines. Think of more ways and means to use your own wisdom and your own philosophy. And use your own attitude, your own faith, your own courage, your own commitment, your own desires, your own excitement. Invest it in discipline so it's not wasted.

5. DEVELOP THE ABILITY TO SHARE.

Pass along to others what you've learned. If you've picked up a good idea while reading this book, pass it along. Don't let it die on the vine. Pass it along. Share your ideas, experiences, knowledge, and you can have just as much pleasure as I do. I make the best investment I can of words and spirit and heart and soul and time and energy. I don't have to work this hard. But I gladly work this hard. Why? I want the return. The people who write or call me—their words touch my life. You can't buy that feeling with money.

Share with your children, share with your colleagues, share with everybody who comes within your grasp. Sharing not only helps you, it helps the other person too. It also makes you bigger than you are. If you're full of ideas and good things, I'm asking you to pour it out. Human beings have an unlimited ability to grow in consciousness and awareness and capacity. Start pouring—and start living a good, ripe life.

THE FOUR IFs

I was asked to give a talk to a service club, and I came up with the topic, "The Four Ifs That Make Life Worthwhile." I will pass it along to you for your consideration and perhaps you will want to share it with others (tell them where you got it, please).

The four ifs that make life worthwhile:

1. LIFE IS WORTHWHILE IF YOU CONTINUE TO LEARN.

Your own experience can be a great teacher. Look back over your life for the past three to six years—you've probably been doing it right or been doing it wrong. Six years is a pretty good chunk of time to go over and evaluate and put it on the scales and see if you are on track or off track. Learn from what you see by evaluating your own experience.

Another way to learn is from other people's experiences. If someone had an excellent, tragic, or life-changing experience and wrote a book about it—and you could read the book in five days—wouldn't that be an advantage? This is the extraordinary kind of learning and skills necessary to gain the high life treasures. It's a small price to pay for treasure—the extra reading, the extra commitment to the excellence of learning. Life is worthwhile if you continue to learn.

2. LIFE IS WORTHWHILE IF YOU TRY.

You have to try and see what you can do with your life. How do you know where you're going if you don't try to get there? How do you know if you will win the game, the disagreement, the promotion—how do you know if you don't try? I urge you to make a commitment to try.

Set goals; set your bar a little higher than you think you can reach. Then try! Take a run at it. I don't know any other way to get ahead. How do you know if you can make it to the next hurdle if you don't try? Keep trying. Try again. Try it over. Try it another time. Try it another way. Try it with more speed. There are all kinds of ways to try—and succeed.

3. LIFE IS WORTHWHILE IF YOU STAY.

You have to learn to hang in there no matter the circumstances. Learn to stay through the thick and thin of life. Don't be a quitter—there's no knowing what is on the other side of a challenge if you give up in the middle of it.

To win, you must stay in the game (of life). Just because you're behind in the first quarter, don't leave. Hang in there. Build a foundation and then stay throughout the construction process. Stay as the walls go up and the roof goes on. Hang in there—it worth it.

4. LIFE IS WORTHWHILE IF YOU CARE.

Caring is an important human value. If you care at all, you'll get results. If you care enough, you'll get incredible results. Care for each day and use its time wisely. Care for people and help them with their possibilities. Care for the enterprise—its dignity and reputation. And care for yourself—to become all you can become, stretch as far as you can stretch, accomplish as much as you can accomplish. Have something good to say.

TODAY I'M WEALTHY

I gave a speech and the title was "Today I'm a Wealthy Man." Didn't have much to do with money, but here's what I said:

> I'm wealthy because of my heritage. My parents, my grandparents. My grandmother studied nutrition, passed it on to my mother. Back in those days when my mother studied and practiced nutrition, she was called a health nut because she was studying vitamins. Mama mixed up some stuff for me and Papa said, "If this don't kill us, I think it'll help." We gagged it down. With the practice and study of better nutrition, Mama extended her life at least 20 years, the doctor told her. My father lived to be 93 and never had a major illness. I've never had a major illness either and I passed on that heritage to my children, my grandchildren. My heritage. What's that worth? It's worth a fortune. So contemplate your blessings every once in a while, and part of your blessing is your heritage.

Next is the heritage of your country. We who come from the free countries can engage in enterprise to start with a dollar and make a fortune; we can become millionaires. What value is that heritage? It's unbelievably tremendous. We enjoy the benefit of courts we didn't start. We enjoy the benefit of laws we didn't create. We enjoy the benefit of learning institutions we didn't found. We enjoy the benefit of medicine we didn't discover. We are wealthy in myriad ways.

I'm a wealthy man because of my experiences. Experience makes you rich. You must treat your experiences as commodity. You must treat your experiences as high value. You must treat your experiences as capital so that you can invest in the future, what you've learned in the past. My experiences now have taken me around the world. And I enjoyed a birthday celebration last year in 16 cities. It was one of the most unbelievable experiences of my life. A group got together in Italy and gave me a helicopter tour of cities including Sorrento, Naples, Vesuvius, the Isle of Capri, and Pompeii from the air. Incredible experiences.

Next, I'm wealthy because of my friends—one of the greatest wealths of all, friendship.

I'm wealthy because of what I've learned from the people who have taught me. From the Earl Shoaffs of the world and others who have made a contribution to my intellectual discovery. Those who have helped me refine the track I live on for good health, prosperity, for all the valuable things. We can't put a price tag on someone's book or a conversation, someone who gives you knowledge when you need it the most. When you can't think of the ideas, your head is so clouded maybe with despair, and the clouds of difficulty hover near, this is when you need somebody to whisper valuable information in your ear that helps you to survive and then to finally succeed.

What is that knowledge worth? What is friendship worth? What's a book full of wisdom worth? Someone says $19.95. Say, no, no. That's what it costs to buy it. That's what it costs for the cover and the ink and the pages and the words and getting it to you and all the stuff in between. That's the $20. But you couldn't pay for the ideas—they're free.

Never begrudge the money you spend on personal education. If you keep developing your mind and your perception and your awareness and your ability to discover, the fortune is yours. The health is yours. The promise is yours. A good family relationship is yours. Friendship is yours. Everything is yours if you keep accelerating your education. The best money you can invest is in your personal self-education.

Next, I'm a wealthy man because of my future. I have the wealth and the resources to do anything I want to do. Do you know how amazing that is?

When you take care of navigating toward your future, you will be amazed too.

Lastly, I'm a wealthy man because of unique love experiences. A major share of what I am today came from a unique blended family experience of a love affair unmatched.

Now in closing, I ask you to consider these four questions. I call them questions to ponder.

The first question is **why?** Why should you try? Why get up so early? Why work that hard? Why read so many books? Why make that many friends? Why go that far? Why earn that much? Why give so much away? Why put yourself through all those disciplines?

The best answer I know to the question why is the second question to ponder: **Why not?** What else are you going to do with your life? Why not see how far you can go, how much you can earn or read or share? Why not see what you can become or how far you can go? Why not? You have to stay here until you go. Why not?

The third question goes a bit deeper. **Why not you?** Some people have done the most incredible things with a limited start. Why not you? Some people do so well, they get to see it all. Why not you? Why not you watching the morning mist rise over the mountains of Scotland? Soaking up history in London? Or exploring the mysteries of Spain?

Why not you having lunch in one of those neat little sidewalk cafés in Paris? There's nothing like a stroll through the palace of Versailles. Someday you must gaze directly at the Mona Lisa. Why not you on a sailing schooner in the Caribbean? Two weeks there and you lose all your cares. I can show you where to find the most exquisite seashells in Australia. I know where they are. Why not you? Why not you shopping on Fifth Avenue in New York City staying at the Waldorf? Or having sliced roast goose on a bed of apple strudel at Luchow's?

Stop off and drink in an Arizona sunset. Take a quiet walk along the beach with that incredible feeling knowing you are enjoying the result of a disciplined effort. Why not you with an unusual awareness to the heartbeat of life? Why not you?

The last question is the key to action. **Why not now?** Why postpone your better future any longer? Get at it today. Get some new books. Make a new plan. Set a new goal. Ask some new questions. Lock onto a new resolve. Make a new effort and do it all now.

A FEAST OF IDEAS

Throughout this book, we have shared a feast of ideas that can, if you digest those ideas, satisfy our lifelong desire for both wealth and happiness. Here's what I offer as a suggestion now that we've feasted on the philosophical side, the theory side of the fundamentals. Let me encourage you to participate in what should always follow any feast—activity, exercise, and effort.

In this case, the active and intense application of all that you've learned and shared together. I appeal to you right now to go to work. I appeal to you to review your associations with the people around you. I appeal to you to set your goals, to begin the quest for developing yourself, and to embark on a journey leading to your own financial independence by following a well-defined plan.

I appeal to you to enjoy your life as you seek to improve it. I give to you my strong appeal to seek knowledge so that your value to yourself and to others may increase. Work on all these areas, but by all means work. It is always easier to think than to do. It is easier to promise than to achieve. It is easier to pretend than to produce. It is easier to plan than to act.

I ask you not to do what is easy, but to do what will actually bring you the achievements you seek. Don't be one of those who enjoy wealth but not happiness, those who are happy but not prosperous, or those who are neither happy nor wealthy and seem to ignore some or all of the fundamentals we've discussed.

They are perhaps too busy, too tired, too preoccupied, too lazy, and perhaps even too rich to give attention to the basics. But don't let that be you. Go to work today on the fundamentals and commit yourself to yourself. The results will be well worth it. I promise.

This is my final appeal.

Go do something remarkable.

CONCLUSION

NIGHTINGALE-CONANT

You've just read and absorbed a tremendous amount of wisdom, insight, and information, all of it charged with the power to permanently change your life for the better. But will it? That is the critical question, and the only person who can answer it is you. As any star athlete will tell you, the real power and strength lies in the follow-through.

Many people who read books such as this one never ultimately see the true rewards. It's not because the book's information was inadequate or couldn't deliver. It's because at some point along the way, the reader abandoned the process. Life sometimes, as it does with all of us, just gets in the way. It can crowd out our truest heart's desires.

People who experience this often start out feeling much as you probably do right now. Excited, motivated, dedicated, ready to make the changes needed to reach the goals and achieve the dreams they've set forth for themselves by reading this life-changing book.

That's probably why they purchased it in the first place. The first week after finishing the book goes great. They're shouting from the rooftops that this is it. This is the time that the change will be permanent. They found the answer. But as the days and weeks go by, enthusiasm dies down. The vision fades, and the old habits creep back in.

Maybe life deals them a blow or setback and the goals they originally set for themselves take a backseat. And maybe over time they get forgotten completely. The book gets put on a shelf and pretty soon they're right back where they started. It's simply human nature.

Very few people have the extraordinary level of discipline it takes to be exclusively self-motivated. The rest of us need ongoing, interactive encouragement, support, and motivation if we are going to maintain our enthusiasm and really reach our goals. Without that, it can be impossible to remain focused and on track.

At this moment, you're probably feeling excited, inspired, motivated, empowered, and most importantly, ready to apply the information you've just read. We at Nightingale-Conant want you to keep that feeling going today, tomorrow, and for the rest of your life. And use it to create the life of your dreams. But we know that's not always easy to do, so we encourage you to visit our website where there are many varied resources to help you to continue your progress to become the person you want to be, to live the life you dream of, and reach the goals you plan on achieving. So your life unfolds exactly the way you want it to.

Take action now and you'll change your personal, professional, and financial future immediately and forever. Don't wait until the challenges of life creep back in and keep you from doing what you were truly meant to do. Promise yourself to follow through now.

Visit Nightingale-Conant at nightingale.com for a comprehensive library of life-changing resources from well-known world leaders in personal development. Also available from Sound Wisdom at soundwisdom.com.

ABOUT JIM ROHN

(1930-2009)

For more than 40 years, Jim Rohn honed his craft like a skilled artist—helping people worldwide sculpt life strategies that expanded their imagination of what is possible. Those who had the privilege of hearing him speak can attest to the elegance and common sense of his insights and wisdom.

So it is no coincidence that he is still widely regarded as one of the most influential thinkers of our time and thought of by many as a national treasure. He authored numerous books and audio and video programs and helped motivate and shape an entire generation of personal-development trainers and hundreds of executives from America's top corporations.

GET ALL 3 BOOKS
AND TAKE CONTROL
OF YOUR LIFE!

Available everywhere books are sold.

THANK YOU FOR READING THIS BOOK!

If you found any of the information helpful, please take a few minutes and leave a review on the bookselling platform of your choice.

BONUS GIFT!

Don't forget to sign up to try our newsletter and grab your free personal development ebook here:

soundwisdom.com/classics